Miss Kitty's Saloon

and other works

Cookie Crumbles

Cookie Crumbles

ACKNOWLEDGEMENT

The author wants to thank the following
for their help and kind words in
producing this book:
Robert Klein Engler
Timothy State
Marc Fraizer
Sue Powers

art work by the author

Cookie Crumbles

Table of Contents

Poetry

Performance Pieces

Short Stories

.6.

Cookie Crumbles

Poetry

"Stairway"

Cookie Crumbles

Cookie Crumbles

SHECAGO

[Dedicated to H Rider Haggard]

My senses reel in her excess.
I can't deny her slightest whimcommand.
While I am with her there is no else!
Black furry fog envelopes me.
As the sparkle of broken glass
In moonlight draws me deeper
Toward the shadows and folds
Of the Night World
Where lifedeath simply is --
Never justified.
Riding the El,
Watching the swells
And all the rest
Rubbing shoulders
For my amusement.
I feast at the banquet
Of her largesse
And in mourning morning,
Sordid blood is on her hands
And I forgive her.

Cookie Crumbles

Ode To A Vampyre

wind
walks the cliff.
while,
silence holds my
tongue, as stiff

as
frozen grass.
she
comes into sight
dressed for mass.

she
rims the sea,
each
pink dawning day,
haunting me.

her
god awaits
her
genuflection.
are there fates

worse
than death, in
this
world of shadow?
without sin

Cookie Crumbles

yet
she's condemned,
by
the nature of
my passion.

while
my eye fills
my
heart to bursting,
thoughts of kills

past,
yet to be,
twist
my empty soul.
i must flee!

blood,
warm and thick,
drips
from my fingers
as i lick

cold
white skin. my
teeth
have been stained red,
as i cry.

Cookie Crumbles

while
 the snow creaks
 'neath
 my feet. steam vents.
 air reeks

with
 her death scent.
 in
 my lust, i am
 radiant.

biker boy

fate twists logic to pretzels.
for months I'd vainly searched
the clubs and danced and danced.
i knew him in my unseeing sight.
black denim & leather & oil & gas,
a low-rider.
and under his T, a smooth chest, no bulging
muscles to mar his lines.
and just my height, lip to lip.
short.
short blond casual hair.
so as i walk away from the demo
he breaks out of my gray matter hotel
and thrusts an ACT-UP flyer into my hands
and...i'm speechless...and he melts away.

Cookie Crumbles

The Last Wizard Prince

How came I, lost, to this place?
And the Shining Path--now dark
In fear I sweat blood.

As I seek the cutting edge --
The Flaming Maze, the promise
Of pain, the gift of knowledge.

I thirst, with only Loki's
Piss to slake it. His laughter --
Falling--shatters at my feet.

Binary logic fails me.
Lost in these lands of shadow,
A thin sliver of the One.

The champion eternal
Exiled from communion
Stripped of that power.

Of that hideous strength,
My hand gripped the Singing Sword.
But that Sword has gone missing.

While I possessed my right hand
And the Singing Sword keened the
Song of my fathers' fathers.

Cookie Crumbles

Fought battles across every
 Earth--in league with Man--I sought
 The end of the Magicians.

 The inconsolable souls
 I drained of life hector me
 As I wander this cursed plane.

 Trapped--as if I were human--
 Unable now to transpose
 Reality for my will.

Cookie Crumbles

Transitions

A shrine to a moving picture house, how odd…
A jewel, years beyond its glory days,
Yet it appeared on many screens playing itself.
A shrine on Thalia Street in New Orleans.
All that remains is the intricate tile of the lobby floor
And the curved stairs that led to the magic place.
It was not the waters of Katrina that took her away.
It was a fire--it roared through and left her in ashes.
The five stairs held flowers and stuffed animals
A broken TV at the center of it's arc held a toy fire truck.
The Coliseum Theater lives only in still pictures now.

Cookie Crumbles

River Bank

Sedimentary stone steps
Provide perfect seats to see
the upper pool lap at the infinite edge.

Below, unmatched slabs of stone
find water cutting through the cracks
and dancing, ledge to ledge.
The lower pool fills a shallow gorge.

A yellow sun hangs low.
Balanced on the knife-edge of change
the trees glow golden in the warm air.

The cool forest breeze raises, for just
A moment, hairs on the back of my neck.

Cookie Crumbles

Jacking the Moon

Was that a stop sign flying by?
A dip in the road brings riverine air
But the shivers aren't from that
You say you're seventeen.
You say you're a girl.
And I'm willing to believe
Feeling your arms so tight
Round my leathers
I'll just close my eyes.
And feel your presence.
As the howling wind guides me
Riding in the dark with headphones

Cookie Crumbles

Performance Pieces

Cookie Crumbles

Cookie Crumbles

"Pinwheel"

Cookie Crumbles

Cookie Crumbles

Dorm Life Off Campus

Ms Crumbles takes the stage in zebra print miniskirt, black tank top, black boots and MC jacket and BIG hair

{Intro music: first 10 seconds of Shape of Things to Come}

[Enter from rear of theater, circuit Stage looking for chair. Wave, nod wink etc. Sit in chair and place purse on floor]

Nineteen sixty-eight is a year that many people judge harshly because they're hung up on '67, you know, the Summer of Love and all that Peace Love and Understanding. Well, like Osgood says at the end of the movie "Some Like It Hot", nobody's perfect!

[Stand up]

In 1968 me and Tommy had been living together ever since they sent him home from Vietnam. He'd dropped out of high school and joined the Marines when we were Seniors. Been gone about a year when--suddenly-- he showed up on my doorstep. Said he couldn't go home. [Walk to Outer Stage Left] I never asked what happened in the jungle…and he never told me. I was in college and he was just hangin', we bounced from apartment to apartment in the hippie section of Madison.[Lean toward audience, like in confidence] I'm not really proud of this, but we were into sticking it to the man. We would pay the first month's rent and the security deposit.

After that it was catch as catch can…eventually we'd get the eviction notice and find someplace else. It seemed there was an infinite supply of dumpy apartments that may or may not have had heat but they sure had

Cookie Crumbles

rodents! We'd pretend the big ones were squirrels. We didn't figure to create a commune it just worked out that way.

[Walk to Outer Stage Right]

One morning we were coming home around daybreak and found Butch sitting next to our steps,

[look down]

trying to look inconspicuous. Butch was an outlaw, of the mild not wild variety. He was Tommy's cousin and had recently escaped from kiddie prison. He even had a tattoo; he was so skinny--not at all macho.

[Walk Stage Center]

After Butch settled in with us he hooked up with his girlfriend T'sa--proof--he wasn't the sharpest knife in the drawer, she being only fifteen. But T'sa was a real-life Lolita

[Lean down, stroking boobs out, face right]

--always got what she wanted. Butch worshipped her--which is why he ended up in kiddie prison in the first place. T'sa would show up at our apartment at 8 o'clock in the morning announcing that she was "boozing" school. Boozing school…I'd never heard anyone call it that before. So, there we were, [gesture chest, left, right, grimace] me, Tommy, Butch and T'sa. Then,

[Sit down R hand R knee--L hand chair back straight up]

Cookie Crumbles

Christine enters the picture. Tommy was spending a lot of time on the phone with her--his Ex. They had dated all though junior high but her family had moved away after graduation and he'd never seen her again. She was the first person he'd called when he got back to the world. He was ecstatic to find out she didn't have a boyfriend. After Tommy generated a phone bill with three digits, she finally agreed to come to the city for a visit.

So, all five of us--Tommy, Christine, Butch, T'sa & me--ended up living in a one-bedroom apartment where the bedroom was paved with wall-to-wall mattresses. We were all very comfortable.

[Stand up]

We had a major blowout the night Christine decided she'd stay at our little Hog Farm, the 20-watt stereo with the swing-down turntable and the detachable speakers was cranked up with Hendrix and Cream--just pounding away. The party was actually in full-throated roar when I got home from my part-time gig at the KFC--loaded down with two buckets of liberated chicken.

[Show chicken]

When I asked where Butch and T'sa were, Tommy pointed to the bathroom. I needed to relieve myself so I moved toward the door. [move Outer Stage Left] T'sa's head popped out and she said to come in. Butch had been eating lunch at some burger joint when two cops sat down at the next table. He thought he heard the cop nearest to him mention the Reform School--from which he was a recent dropout. The other one, the one who could see him, was straining to get a look at the tattoo on Butch's neck, a marijuana leaf. Butch got so unnerved, he left his sandwich

Cookie Crumbles

uneaten on the table while he slipped out the back door. Which--according to T'sa--was why Butch was now standing in our bathroom in full drag with platinum blond hair, just like T'sa's and his tattoo covered with panstick. Originally she only planned to cover the tattoo. But once she started--she realized how utterly feminine Butch really was. She figured with blond hair and the right makeup he could pass for a girl. Maybe even hang out at her Mom's house as her girlfriend.

The only flaw in her plan? He was too scared to come out of the bathroom.So T'sa wanted me to get in drag to give him some cover. Wow! No one knew that I was a closet case. I'd been missing my dress up sessions since I left home the previous year and here they were--telling me to get all dolled up! Not a hard sell, but I didn't want to appear too eager, {beat} so I made Butch beg me...I agreed and ten minutes later T'sa left to announce the fabulous floorshow!

[Do floor show Center Stage all the way to Stage REAR--manic]

Everyone was slack-jawed at the sight of Butch all dragged out looking damn fine I might add. I wasn't nearly as cute as he was but we wanted to put on a good show! As soon as we hit the living room Butch lost every inhibition he might have had. T'sa had told us to do a bump and grind.

So we did it, back to back, asses grinding, going down to the floor and back up. We were really getting the partygoers crazed –- a lot of chemicals had been consumed in that room.

Everyone started clapping and then somebody, not sure who exactly, demanded that we "girls" face each other and french kiss. T'sa thought that it was just the best idea ever! She told Butch to do it and well, like I said before, Butch did whatever T'sa said. I was pleasantly surprised to find

Cookie Crumbles

that it wasn't any different from frenching a girl. So much so that I was getting into it in a big way. Butch didn't seem to mind either.

The party got really LOUD! Every time Butch and I tried to break it off, the hooting, hollering and stomping would reach a manic crescendo. At the peak I swear I saw the apartment door bulge off its hinges!

Tommy answered it and two big burly cops barged in. At first I didn't see them as I had my eyes closed. The music suddenly stopped. One of the cops tossed a piece of chicken from the bucket in the kitchen at the turntable. Knocked the needle right off the record. That got my attention. I still had my arm around Butch's waist as the bigger cop walked over to us.

"Is your name Theresa Kalinsky?" the cop asked Butch.

If Butch hadn't been totally painted up he would have been whiter than our refrigerator. He just shook his head and tried to breathe. I noticed T'sa was sliding off towards the bedroom. So did the other cop. He crossed the room in two steps and grabbed her by the arm. She started screaming bloody murder as the cop put cuffs on her.

The first cop turned his attention back to Butch and me.

"Ah--you two Lezzies can go back to what you were doing…" he said, leering at us.

[Walk to Stage Front Edge]

Now I was starting to freak out. But I figured it was best to play along. Unfortunately, T'sa wasn't about to go down alone, she started screaming for Butch to

Cookie Crumbles

"DO SOMETHING". The cops realized that we were not what we appeared to be and with very little questioning Butch spilled the whole story. The party--was over.

[Sit down]

Turns out that T'sa had been bragging to all her girlfriends that she was living with a bunch of hippies

downtown, one of their mothers called T'sa's house and ratted her out... So T'sa went home to Mom, poor Butch went back to kiddie prison, eventually Tommy and Christine got married.

[Pick up purse, stand, move to steps]

...Oh and me? I caught a long...long ride on the crazy train.

{Close with 15 seconds of Ozzie Osborne's Crazy Train on "...crazy train".}

END OF SCENE

Cookie Crumbles

A Girl's Night Out

Setting: A woman sits, back to the audience, stage left. There is an abstract representation of a man, stage right. The woman [still sitting] stretches and rises to her feet. She [obviously] resets her wig on her head. She is wearing a black slip. She turns to the audience, yawns and walks to center stage, opens her purse [sets purse on box] and removes a lipstick. She plays with it as she begins to speak, to the man.

I just love sex, don't you? I mean it's just so utterly ethereal, I often feel like I've left my body and I'm floating away. Is it the same for you? To be honest I was surprised that we hooked up last night, you're not really my type, too bulky and hairy, but you came on so strong--you simply swept me away. I haven't been to a dance club in ages. But since I just came back to town I figured why not, for old times sake, you know? I saw you staring at me as soon as I walked in the club, you were so obvious, but then I guess that's your style.

You do have that masculine presence that so many girls adore. I mean I do understand it, sometimes it's just so nice to surrender volition, take leave of responsibility--let yourself become that little leaf floating downstream without a care. Normally I'm much more inclined to the cuddly teddy bear type of guy, not nerdy exactly, but somewhat less worldly, certainly much less so than a man of action like yourself. As soon as I felt your cock swelling against my belly, well, I just have to say, this girl LIKES to be appreciated.

I don't know what it is about tranny chasers, what drives them? I don't like to be judgmental, but you know a lot of them are just the worst kind of trolls and they simply don't treat a lady the way she deserves to be treated. Your being courteous scored a lot of points with me. Sometimes

Cookie Crumbles

these assignations end abruptly when my suitor finds I've had the final cut, so I was glad to hear that you did not mind my having a front-loaded pussy.

Too bad you didn't meet me in my prime, I mean I'm kinda thick though the middle now; but I wasn't always. I got heavy in my late twenties--in my teens I was short, well I'm still short...but I was very thin--I was always going out dressed, my father was on the road a lot and my mother was a hostess in a fancy cocktail lounge on weekends, she ran the wait staff so she had fabulous clothes I could borrow. By the time I was thirteen my little brother was eight; she'd drop him off at grandma's house and pick him up on Sunday. For some reason she didn't think I'd get into trouble on my own.

As soon as I was certain she wouldn't be back for a comb or a different pair of earrings, I'd slip into a miniskirt, ankle-strap pumps and a tank top. With the proper padding I could easily pass for sixteen. I kept my hair down to my shoulders; I was fairly blond back then. I'd go to the mall or the movies and flirt outrageously with the boys I'd meet. I was as happy as a girl like me could be. Life was sweet--for a while.

As they say, I was riding for a fall. One of the neighbor ladies who had too much time on her hands was taking note of the cute little hottie coming and going from our house, she took it into her head that this little slut was taking advantage of me, being that she was so obviously older than me. One weekend she ran into my dad at the local grocery store and filled him in on her suspicions...so he decided to catch us in the act.

The next Friday he got someone to cover for him and he came home to bust my phantom sweetie doing the nasty, what he busted was me--sitting at my mother's vanity, wearing a lacy slip over my favorite Victoria's Secret

Cookie Crumbles

bra and panty set. I was almost finished painting myself into that girl I loved to be.

As he entered the bedroom I felt the heat of his anger and disgust rush ahead of his steps, there was no young trollop here. Only his son birthing a girl! He was livid, he told me not to move as he stormed out of the room returning shortly with an almost full bottle of Jack Daniels. He sat on the bed as he drank freely from the bottle and had me doing pirouettes after donning a pair of spike heels taller than I'd ever worn before. He kept asking me if I sucked cock, and if I was a girl--why not?

I was crying, wailing really. I begged him to let me change clothes, swearing I'd never do it again. He took a knife out of his pocket and flicked it open; the overhead light gleamed off the immaculate blade. He pointed it at me and asked me if I wanted to be a girl right now. I screamed NO--more scared than I'd ever been in my life. He told me he could take my nuts in an instant and no one would care. I cried harder. He drank more.

He stood up and moved towards me I had no idea what was coming next. He grabbed me by my hair and began to slice it from my skull. This shearing went on forever, I stopped crying, eventually. When my mother came home I was sitting in the middle of her bed, my hair hacked off, my scalp seeping blood from nicks and cuts, too terrified to move a centimeter.

When she stopped screaming my father demanded to know why she was letting me dress like a girl, run around town, have sex with boys…She told him that she knew I'd never be a real boy and she didn't see the harm in my acting like a girl. I was going to end up as one anyway. My father roared that he'd never accept that and he meant it.

Cookie Crumbles

The next morning I found myself on the way to military school. My father had made some calls to old buddies from his army days. I never lived with my family again. From military school I went into the army, brainwashed I guess you could say. My father thought that short hair and a uniform would cure me of being a girl, HAH, not according to Army Intelligence. In spite of my father's phobic reaction to my femininity the Army spooks found my sexual identity a real asset. They said I appealed to a certain subset of men, from whom they wanted me to extract information. They paid for my sojourn in Thailand. But all those years away from home came at a price. I never got to know my brother and I only communicated with Mom via e-mail. I was living a movie, a blonde American T-girl--in high demand in Southeast Asia and I was able to deliver the goods my agency coveted.

My baby brother Conrad turned out to be every bit the same kind of girly girl I was, only a LOT prettier. Mom finally left dad because he went nuts when he discovered that he sired two little, as he put it, faggots! Once away from my father's pernicious influence Conrad blossomed into Connie, the junior miss. Mom did everything she could to raise him as a proper young lady.

But Mom lost the genetic lottery and by the time Connie was 19 my mother was dying of ovarian cancer. I didn't even find out about it until I concluded the mission I was executing; but by then she'd been dead for months. Without Mom's steadying hand Connie just went off the deep end, she had all that insurance money--bought herself a pair of magnificent boobs--she became a monumental party girl. But the party ended--the night she met you.

So I guess I should tell you that you are one good fuck. Kinda funny

Cookie Crumbles

really. One more conflict for you to ponder at your last moment. When I raked your back with my talons, filed to a ginsu edge, I drew blood, lots of blood. I did worry a bit about how to keep you under control. I certainly did not want this to end badly, for me that is. Luckily I am well versed in this particular technique.

Curare is very interesting; I wanted you awake but not able to move. I had to take quite a risk, too much and your ability to breathe would cease and then we would never be able to have had this lovely chat, because I simply had to tell you everything and I wanted to watch your eyes.

[Pick up the duct tape and hold it so the audience can see it. Pull it out with as much noise as possible and walk over to the killer.]

What did you say? What? DON'T TALK, JUST LISTEN!

[Affix the duct tape to the mouth, two strips]

There--much better, can't hear a thing now…

[Remove a big hair clip from the purse, flex it a few times and attach it to the second knuckle of your left hand.]

Ow, that hurts!

[Walk to the killer.]

I think you'll have at least a minute, maybe two while you try to suck air through that thick layer of duct tape before you black out.

I hope you think about why you decided to kill her. Your pathetic excuse

Cookie Crumbles

at the trial, the 'I didn't know she had a dick' defense, what a joke! I think you just like to kill T-girls. Did you plan to beat me to death like you did Connie? Well--whatever--you got off with a lousy five years. As I waited for you to get out I had a long time to think about how I'd make you pay for your crime. You took my sister away from me and now your atonement begins.

[Put the clip on his nose.]

GO to BLACKOUT

END OF SCENE

Cookie Crumbles

Look Homeward Dairy Queen

Scene 1: Bathroom

An empty picture frame is held in the air.
A brunette walks up in a bathrobe, carrying toothbrush.
Starts brushing teeth in the mirror.

Voiceover: Well, today is my anniversary! I can't believe another year has slipped away from that very special night. The thrill of victory as I accepted the acclaim of my fans! Like every little drag queen--I knew I was worthy of a crown--it seems so close I could reach out and touch it…

(She stops brushing and reaches out to her image.)

Blackout.

Scene 2: Coronation

She stands revealed as the lights go up: gown, blonde hair, and tiara,
holding bouquet of roses and the winner's sash across her chest.

"Thank you, thank you. I'm overwhelmed--I can't believe I've won. When I lost the swimsuit competition AND the talent competition I never dreamed my little essay "Cheese--the Foundation of Civilization" would be so strong. Go Cheddar!I promise to be the very best Queen that Wisconsin has ever seen!!" I understand that along with this great honor I also I have a great duty to bring peace and prosperity to the world or at least South East Wisconsin.

Cookie Crumbles

Scene 3: To the Dells

Phone rings.

She turns her back to the audience and removes receiver from the table. A sign on her back says "Three Months Later". "What? Tonight? I can't possibly get there in time. They'll fly me out of Timmerman Field? Well--that's different. OK. Give me the details again. I need to be at Cappy Wick's Cheezz Torte in Wisconsin Dells at 9 PM. OK then."

Blackout

Scene 4: Limo at Dick's [as if at a car window]

"Driver, Mr. Limo Driver! You're certain this place is Cappy Wick's Cheezz Torte?? It looks kinda out of the way here in the middle of the dark woods. You're sure? Uh huh... And you'll be back to pick me up?"

[turns to audience]

I watched as the car roared off with a rooster tail of gravel. Well it turns out that it wasn't Cappy Wick's Cheezz Torte, it was Capt Dick's Gay Resort. The bartender said they were in dire straits as the MC for the annual amateur strip show hadn't shown up and according to him I looked to be exactly the girl they needed to fill in for her! I went to the bathroom to freshen up for my duties as the Carol Merrill of beefcake and--I couldn't believe my eyes--there, tuning up her mascara at the bathroom mirror, was my classmate from the University of Wisconsin--Milwaukee, Ginger Gagnon . We were in all the same classes that semester. She told me that her friend Gloria had brought her to Capt Dick's to help her get over her broken heart. Why is it that the sweetest girls always have such miserable

Cookie Crumbles

cads for boyfriends? She said that Gloria and her were sharing a cabin just past the little bubbling brook across from the main lodge and invited me to stay overnight. I told her that my limo was due back by midnight, but I thanked her kindly. The strip show was more fun than any of the milk and cheese contests I had previously judged in my official capacity as the Dairyland Queen. In fact I have to say that I took a--possibly--unfair interest in one of the contestants as I held my hand above the head of each hunky young man invoking the fevered applause of the audience. The two finalists were equally adorable…but MY favorite won--somehow…To my great disappointment none of the strippers seemed to have any interest in girls, not even a bona fide crowned queen such as myself. As charming as I am I took my leave. I knew that I would not be in the running for their after hours plans. Which is how I came to be standing at the pool table watching three thirty-something guys playing--at a skill level that didn't intimidate me. They needed a fourth to fill out partners and asked me if I played pool.

I played way over my head--me and my partner, his name was Bruce--won three games in a row and all the hooting and hollering attracted the attention of Ginger and Gloria. Ginger hadn't yet hooked up. They walked over about the time the bartender announced last call--which made me suddenly realize that my limo never came back. As we left the bar--Bruce, looking right at Ginger--asked if we girls would like to come by their cabin for a glass of bubbly or two. We said umm--sure! The boy's suite was deluxe. It was hot men and cold Champaign all the way. A huge red Jacuzzi with four jets of atomic scrubbing bubbles dominated the front room, there was a big overstuffed love seat and two comfy wing chairs facing the tub. I haven't been in a room full of naked men since High School and I wasn't wearing a evening gown with four inch pumps then, although I certainly wanted to be! Two of the boys were watching the tub fill up while Bruce languidly lay on the love seat. His little soldier was

Cookie Crumbles

ready for sentry duty. But Miss Gagnon was in the boy's shower tripping off her paint and I--in a moment of weakness--fell on Bruce. He was a comfortable mouthful, not the sort of thing that wakes you up in the middle of the night with lockjaw.

The shower noise finally stopped and Miss Gagnon appeared behind me and said "Heyyyyyy" speaking volumes in that single elongated syllable...Being dedicated to public service, I relinquished the barely used beef jerky. However, loath to be a mere bystander--I moved up to his right nipple...I tugged at Gloria's sleeve and she joined in on his left nipple. We made a lovely geometric figure. Two bejeweled, high-heeled drag queens topside and the freshly scrubbed Miss Gagnon--once more all boy--working the fire down below. All the clenching, moaning, writhing tight overhead money shot that a first rate porno director could have asked for--had there been one! After a time the splashing and giggling in the hot tub drew our attention. Gloria and I rolled off Bruce's chest and Miss Gagnon took hold of her beau--and returned to the sea as it were. Since the four boys were naked and wet and getting wetter Gloria and I sat in the two comfy wing chairs and settled in for the show. Sadly there was no popcorn. So we contented ourselves with holding up score cards like Olympic judges.

[hold up big white scorecards]

Nothing less than a 9.9--of course. After a while--long enough--we looked at each other and said "Our work here is done..." They never even noticed we were gone.

END OF SCENES

Cookie Crumbles

100% Human Hair

SET:
A desk.
A phone.
A make-up mirror.
A box of earrings.
Blonde Dolly wig on the wighead.
A purse [with cell phone]
Sitting in the dark.

*[The light in the mirror goes on. Stage lights come up.
I touch up my lipstick.]*

[I'm reaching for my hair as...]

SOUND CUE:
The phone rings.

[I put the hair back and answer, right hand.]

COOKIE: What's up Glory? Tonight? I'd love to--really, but I can't. Nope. Gotta work. No, not all night. Goddess knows, I can't do that anymore. But if I get done early...Where was I last night? I did not stand you up. No, cause I NEVER planned on meeting you. I had dinner plans with Charlie. Well no...I didn't, um, he called and canceled. Yeah, again. Oh--he is NOT an asshole!

[Holding various earrings to her ear]

Cookie Crumbles

He has a lot of commitments, that's all. His daughter called late. She needed him to pick her up at the college. Yes, for the whole weekend.

[Pause]

Boyfriend trouble. Her mother is out of town. Europe…{*tempo*} Milan… {*tempo*} Yeah, the new fall line. She'll probably take one of each, the bitch.

[Pause]

No, he CAN'T divorce her. Cause she'd take him for everything he has, he'd end up living here! The jury would give her a dump truck full of cash.

[Pause]

For pain and suffering--her husband being seen in the company of a FABULOUS Drag Queen all over the Quarter--at The Court of Two Sister's brunch for Christ's sake. Well, his wife lost interest long before we met, so I feel noooo guilt.

[Pause]

Oh I can't believe I never told you how I met Charlie. Really! It must be four, almost five years ago now. I took the night off to see a concert. Who? Oh come on, I can't remember what color eye shadow I used today. I was such a dumb ass--Christ knows Security dudes are always off duty cops. Well it was right after I'd gotten my implants,

[Pause]

Cookie Crumbles

uh huh. Probably knocked down my IQ a dozen points. I was wearing my tightest jeans and my spikiest heels. Yeah, perfect for standing in line. I had this glossy wooden trick case. Goddess I wish I still had it! I got it in Chicago, when I used to live in Old Town. It wasn't even a paraphernalia shop, just a tobacconist.

[Pause]

Yeah, that's the one. You had to squeeze it just right and then it swung open in reverse. If you didn't--you could never get it open. Five perfect joints--guaranteed two hit wowie.

[Pause]

Yeah, that shit my brother gets from the botanist in Mad city. I had the box in my rear pocket. The Security guy bitched at me to pull the box out since his beefy fingers wouldn't fit back there.

[Pause]

Oh yeah, very funny, haha…a ring bologna would…So I stalled--trying to think of something to say. Then he says that he's a cop and if I didn't want to get arrested I'd better open the damn box. I said I found it in the street just before I got in the line. I said if he wanted it, it was all his, and I handed it to him! He tried to open it, and he couldn't and got really red in the face. There's like a million thirsty rockers waiting to get in. So he's screaming at me. "Show me how to open it!" When he started talking jail again, the guy behind me said, "Just take the box and let her go, she told you you could have it." That was Charlie. The cop turns on him--really mean now, you know how cops can get when they're embarrassed. "So who are you, her fuckin' lawyer?" And he goes "As a matter of fact I AM

Cookie Crumbles

her attorney." And he gives the cop his card. Too cool. Charlie starts giving the cop heat about not getting the box open, not knowing WHAT'S really inside, no probable cause, yada yada yada. Burying him in lawyer-shit. The cop's eyes rolled up in his head. He must've gotten hammered in court by some real piranha--ya know? He just gave up--waved us on. I couldn't believe it! My hunky white knight steered me into the club leaving the cop standing there like a dick. I was extremely grateful to Charlie and I proved it to him.

[Pause]

Well yeah, besides, he's so easy on the eyes. I never really expected to see him again but a few weeks later he showed up at the coffeehouse on St. Anne's.

[Pause]

Cause I'd mentioned--once--that it was my favorite hangout. And now he just floats in and out of my life…

[Pause]

Very much like a guardian angel, now that you mention it. Listen Glory, I've really got to go, I don't want to be late for work. I know, I do go on and on, don't I? Oh, yeah,--just one more thing…

[Pause]

OK OK, I'll be quick. Do you still collect angels?

[Pause]

Cookie Crumbles

The only person I know with more angels than you is Jim from Hyde Park.

[Pause]

Why am I asking? I was just thinking--if you had one to spare, I saw a guy the other day that sure could have used one. I was at Le Bon Temp for lunch. Yes lunch! I am up before noon, almost everyday as a matter of fact. I was waiting for a client, in the front dining room. All those French doors wide open, the place looked as though the wall was completely missing. Anyway, I was trying to make up my mind about food, either Shrimp Remoulade or Oysters Bienville. I was too hungry to wait for the client; besides food wasn't his main concern. No dear, spinach is Oysters Rockefeller, Bienville is crumb dressing and cheese. Sorry…Suddenly this goofy-ass mime is standing behind my waiter. Yes he was cute, you think they're gonna hire ugly waiters?

[Pause]

Oh the mime--no he wasn't cute, if he was cute he would've been an actor. I didn't see him come in, he just appeared somehow…He's pretending that he's at a window with his nose pressed against the glass-- what is it about mimes? Do you know anyone that is wild about mime? I mean, have you ever heard anyone say, "Oh oh, the new mime show is here! Let's go tonight!"

[Pause]

Well, your cousin Louie also bought Shitake mushrooms on the street in the East Village thinking they were psyllisybin, didn't he? So anyway,

Cookie Crumbles

the mime's using his left hand to suggest the glass and he's wearing this canvas grocery sack thing on his hip. He's moving backwards across the room snatching one croissant from each table's breadbasket and slipping it into his sack. OK?I hear this screeching "Get Out!" and the busboy comes barreling out of the kitchen, shaking his fist in the mime's face. "I told you last time--never come back!" The mime--of course--says

[Pause.]

Right…nothing. This enrages the busboy. He's only half the size of the mime, but he picks him up and chucks him out the french doors, smack into the street.

[Pause.]

He landed on his ass. If he had landed on his head he'd have crushed his melon for sure. It's like a four-foot drop to street level. He seemed stunned, but he never broke character. He got up--brushed off the street dirt with big theatrical gestures. By this time the busboy had returned to the kitchen so he didn't see the mime clamber back into the dining room. And so he stood there--eyes blazing--like a conquering hero or a lunatic. Your choice. My waiter was freaked. He totally forgot me. He tried to shoo the mime back out into the street like some errant pigeon. But the mime would have none of it. He stood his ground…silently. Well--

[Pause]

exactly!

[Pause]

Cookie Crumbles

Just what you would expect...the busboy heard the waiter trying to reason with the crazy mime, spins on his heel...manages to drop the tray of bowls he was carrying with this roaring crash. The waiter and the mime both turn to look at the busboy as he launches a roundhouse kick towards the mime's head. It connects and blood bursts from his white painted nose, the spray nearly reaches my table. The mime goes down. At this point I have completely lost my appetite so I pick up my purse and make my way through the gathering crowd in the street and head up to Good Friends for a stiff drink.

[Pause]

Oh, that's the upstairs bar of course, that boy makes the most wonderful Bloody Mary. He's from some little town in Alabama; and he's got the most attractive...

[Pause]

I was going to say accent, but you're right, very nice ass. I just adore his type you know, that reminds me of the time...[About to launch into another story]

[Pause]

Oh, ...you've got someone on the other line...of course.

OK then, I'll let you go dear. Yes, I absolutely have to work tonight, but if I feel up to it I'll meet you after--at the Pocket. Right, it's strippers tonight--from Montreal I think. Bye. Love you too.

[Hang up the phone. Finally reach out and put my big blonde hair in place

Cookie Crumbles

on my head. Look in the mirror and give it a few brushstrokes. I push back from the desk, stand, stretch...open a desk drawer and take out a laptop. Open it, plug in a jack, boot it up,]

SOUND CUE: "You've got mail"

Cookie: Shit! Virus alert! Oh shit, this is a bad one. Another KLEZ variant. Oh shit. Hope I can access my customer server. Come on, come on, connect--damn you! Oh, I hate modems! Try it again. Failed again. Fuck, I'll have to call the help desk.

[Removes cell phone from purse. Dials]

Song? Huh? Oh, I'm sorry--Is this the System Admin desk? Oh--she's on maternity leave? I didn't even know she was pregnant. OK, and your name is Marlene? Thanks Marlene, this is Four Queens Software Maintenance, uh huh, uh huh, yup, my name is Justine. Should be right there on your authorized list. I'm fine honey, how are you doing tonight? Good. Well I'm having trouble with that modem hanging off the HP cluster on the 4th floor. Again. Yeah, I know, I know they should be networked, but you know how paranoid they are. Do you think you could send someone down there to power cycle that thing--so I can login? I gotta get these security patches installed tonight or they'll have my ass, no excuses, know what I mean? Five minutes? OK honey, thanks so much. I really appreciate the support. You have a good weekend now. Oh, she had a girl? Uh huh. I'll have to send a card.

[Pause]

I'm sorry Marlene, I'd love to chit chat, but I'm on the clock here, gotta go! Thanks again!

Cookie Crumbles

[Pause]

Whew! Lucked out that time.

[Black Out]

Light CUE: Lights off

END OF SCENE

.50.

Short Stories

Cookie Crumbles

Cookie Crumbles

"Hot Dog Party"

Cookie Crumbles

The Raw Bar

I'm eating Japanese solo on Tuesday as my lunch date had stood me up. I'm at the bar I might add; I'd been seated at my regular table, a fourtop, but then I saw three people waiting to sit down. I couldn't be rude so I offered them my table--a spot at the sushi bar had just opened up...and well, I've got a big heart.

Since I'm solo, I'm--how should I put it? FORCED to eavesdrop on the threesome as they sat at my former table. Seems they had just met at some management seminar or something and decided to go to lunch together. They all appeared to be in their mid to late twenties. There was a very cute Asian girl, a black guy [I never did see his face, he had his back to me the whole time] and a central casting wholesome but not too exciting white girl.

Since I could see the two girls I could read their name tags. The Asian girl was named Kiki and the big-boned blonde was Linda. From the conversation I surmised that the guy was named James.

They started off talking about religion. Kiki said she met her family at church every Sunday, Korean Baptist I gathered. Kiki didn't add any details. Linda said she was Polish Xcatholic. The "X" was because when she went to confession, if she got Father Jakowiac behind the screen; as soon as she got to the good stuff he would scream at her, loud enough for everyone in the church to hear, "You did what!". The very last time she had ever gone to church she had taken her mother; since the flu had kept her mom housebound for two weeks she'd missed her weekly penance. The good Father Jakowiac was in the box.

James laughed and said he only went to church on Xmas and Easter cause if he didn't his mother wouldn't let him eat holiday dinner at her house and he'd kill for her mac and cheese.

Anyway, as you would expect, the talk turned from religion to sex. The white girl was talking about her best friend, a boy, but totally platonic -

Cookie Crumbles

every time she asked him for a favor he'd say "That's worth two hummers." Or three, or whatever.

So James says, "...um, did you ever pay off? Did you ever blow 'em?"

She made a face like she had a mouthful of raw eggs and broken shells and she says "No way! I'd figure some other way to pay him off--it was just how we kept score."

"Oh--too bad, hummers are what makes life worth living." James said. "Nine out of ten guys would rather get a BJ than fuck."

Then it got quiet, I had to really strain to hear ;^) and the Asian girl says to James - "...so, do you ever..." and he leans in and says "what?" and she says, "You know...lick, a girl?"

"What! You mean give her a 'mustache ride'?" Said James seeming surprised at Kiki's question. " No, I'm not into that. I send my lady to heaven with my glory stick. My girlfriend wouldn't want it any other way."

"I see," said Kiki. "Well my girlfriend is just the opposite. I've tried to get her interested in a strap-on but she seems determined to wear out my tongue."

At that point a waitress carrying an elaborate three-foot boat with 150 dollars of sushi walked smack into a busboy who was polishing the grain off the table next to the threesome. Arms, legs, and sushi all went flying in three different directions. Sensing the arrival of loads of embarrassment for all concerned I left a 20 on the bar and sidled out the door.

Cookie Crumbles

Swiss Army Disaster

I was up to my armpits in grease. KFC grease. When it wasn't being heated by actual fire it starts to get hard, its natural state. The colonel's joint that I worked in was connected to a burger place. The KFC closed a couple of hours earlier than the restaurant.

This night I was cleaning up after a really brutal dinner rush. I was scraping the burnt grease off the ten burner low boy stove. If you didn't scrape it every night it would get as thick as a glacier before a week was out.

Kathy, the head waitress on nights in the Big Boy restaurant, was leaning against the stainless steel sinks; arms crossed beneath her breasts. I only became aware of her as I raised my head from my scrubbing. Kathy, thick wavy red hair down to her shoulders with green eyes that lifted me to my feet, finally spoke.

"So, you're the new kid?"

"Yeah." I answered eloquently.

Turned out that Kathy had a freaky little fetish. She collected virgin boys like tokens on a charm bracelet. And I had foolishly shared that bit of info with a couple of the burger cooks one night over a mighty fine bong. She told me that if I wanted to cure my affliction that all I needed to do was show up at her place at 0300, just a few hours away.

"Well that sounds fine I said" hoping that the sound of my knees colliding like giant castanets was audible only to me.

See you then she chirped as she spun around and glided away. I rushed to finish my cleanup; I wanted to shower off the smell of fried chicken before I--well, before I went to meet Kathy. I set the door to lock behind me as I went out the back. I threw my leg over my Yamaha and hit the kickstart, as soon as she roared to life I realized that I had to go back in and ask for Kathy's address. That sucked. Lucky for me I could see Jill filling saltshakers in the front booth. She had always seemed to be a

Cookie Crumbles

decent girl, not bitchy at all.

I had hoped that Jill would not smirk quite as broadly as she actually did, but even worse--as I exited the front door with Kathy's address ricocheting in my skull--I saw Jill head over to the shake machine where I expected she'd set the gossip mill to grinding…. me.

A couple hours later found me rocketing down the street, wet hair freezing to my noggin, thinking about removing the onus of virgin from my rap sheet. Kathy greeted me at the door in a football jersey, I watched as she ascended the stairs to her second floor flat. She asked me if I wanted a drink, then popped open two PBRs without waiting for my answer.

I shrugged off my leather jacket [actually borrowed from my roommate, mine had mysteriously vanished the previous week] and looked around the apartment. Kathy grabbed my belt and dragged me towards the bedroom. She tossed off a comment over her shoulder that I had run into a spot of bad luck--as she had just gotten her period. Really? Don't worry about it, she said, most men like a blowjob better than intercourse anyway. At the time I had to take her word for it. Now I guess I don't agree but, I turned out to be a pushy bottom. Know what? The only kind of sex I don't like--is no sex.

I quickly left my clothes in a pile on the floor and we sat on the bed facing each other. I moved in to kiss her but she pushed me away, telling me that she had a boyfriend, so no kissing. Startled, my head spun left to right and back looking around the bedroom as if this was a Hollywood horror movie set or something. She said to chill, he wasn't about to pop out--he was in jail!

She gently pushed me back on the bed and began to pay very sweet attention to my penis. The sensations dwarfed my expectations and eighteen years of anticipation boiled over. I learned a lot about cocksucking that evening. Techniques I've used many times over the years.

A very little bit of small talk followed but I was soon back in the cold

Cookie Crumbles

October night on my way home. In the next weeks Kathy invited me over a couple times. She said that she wanted to make up for just blowing me that first time, I figured I must have been doing something right...I still couldn't get a kiss though. But then the relationship cooled. I assumed she had found a new virgin to deflower. But one bitterly cold night, on a whim, I stopped by. Standing on the porch I saw her doorbell had been pulled out of the doorframe, hanging on by one wire. I pulled out my trusty Swiss Army knife and reconnected the doorbell, then rang it. Bryce, Bryce, her best friend--and never one of my fans--came downstairs, gave me a big smile and told me to come in.

Walking into the kitchen, three of the baddest looking motherfuckers I'd ever seen were sitting at Kathy's table. Now I knew why Bryce had smiled at me...I was going to be the floorshow. I tried to follow Bryce into the living room but the biggest dude stood up and barred my way. He towered over me; his blonde hair was cut in an old-fashioned flattop.

One of the guys at the table twisted around to get a beer out of a cooler on the floor and I saw that the cut-off denim jacket he wore over his leather bore the Skull and Crossed Pistons logo of the Outlaws motorcycle gang. I thought he looked Indian, his jet black hair fell in a braid between his shoulders.

The first words out of the big blonde's mouth sent me reeling. Are you the little punk that's been fucking Kathy? Oh my God! The boyfriend, I'm thinking...I'm thinking I'm seriously dead. One huge beefy hand pushed me up against the door I'd just come through. His other hand suddenly filled with a black leather sap, the kind stuffed with lead, the ugly thing made a sickening slap sound as it bounced off my head. You gonna answer me he asked?

The pain I shoulda felt was missing in action. I was scared but not terrified. The other two guys stood up, one of them said "Hey Jack, take it easy. You gonna kill 'em." I wasn't sure if it was a statement or a question. Jack said, shut up Terry! I became aware of every sound, every motion in

Cookie Crumbles

that room as I calculated my chances of walking out of there.

We're just friends I explained about Kathy and me. We work together at the Big Boy, that's all. You mean that hot dog stand, Jack asked? I said, it's a burger joint, and the sap connected with my skull again. You're a smart ass, ain't 'cha, Jack said.I shook my head contritely, not trusting myself to speak. Where the fuck was Kathy I thought to myself? Maybe she could contribute some little bit of help here? Jack was at least six feet two; his chest was broad enough to display all Ten Commandments, on the original stone tablets. I wondered if he'd read them?Jack grabbed the leather jacket I was wearing. He complimented me on the quality of the leather; asked me where I got it? Could this guy be any more schizoid? I confessed that didn't know, that it was my roommate's jacket.

You know how conflict resolution experts talk about finding common ground??? Not always a good strategy. The guy I lived with, Dale, the one who loaned me the jacket, he was a biker too, he rode with the Spokesmen and as far as I knew they had good relations with the Outlaws, so I told Jack about Dale--ooh not the result I was hoping for.

Jack screamed at me to take it off. He said he knew Dale and Dale would never have given a wimp like me his jacket so I must have stolen it! Damn, how could this keep getting worse? I peeled off the leather and handed it to Jack The other two goons had sat back down as Jack started in again on Kathy and me. I swore that I never had sex with her, that we barely knew each other. Which begged the question of why I was just "dropping in" at three o'clock in the morning.

Kathy and Bryce came running into the kitchen. But I really didn't pay them any attention cause Jack had returned the sap to his left boot and pulled out an overNunder two shot silver derringer from his right boot. He literally put the muzzle between my eyes and told me that I was gonna tell the truth or else. Kathy shouted to leave me alone, that we were just friends and tried to cross the room to me but Terry grabbed her and held her back.

Cookie Crumbles

Jack said that the last thing Kathy's old man had said to him when Jack left the County jail, that morning, was to check up on Kathy and he was damn well sure gonna do that! You know what punk, Jack said, I don't like you! And I don't think anyone would miss you! For some insane reason I was greatly relieved to find that Jack wasn't Kathy's boyfriend

You'll have to take my word for it but things sort of went into slow motion here. The loudest noise I've ever experienced knocked my head back against the door. I figured the top of my head was now gone and blood would momentarily gush into my eyes. I never expected to die like this. I saw Stick--his name was on a patch on his Citgo shirt--jump up so violently that the kitchen table flipped over; through the ringing in my ears I thought I heard him say What the fuck Jack! You wanna go back to jail the same day you got out? I might have been lip reading.

Jack shouted that he shot over my head. Stick grabbed a cast iron skillet off the stove and swung it hard into Jack's elbow, the gun flew into the living room and Jack went down. Stick pulled me away from the door, opened it, picked me up by the back of my belt and threw me down the stairs. I bounced once halfway down, scuttled out across the porch, got on my motorcycle and was gone. I spent the rest of the night huddled under the stairs in the University library basement a few blocks away, being utterly grateful that I was still alive.

Cookie Crumbles

Miss Kitty's Saloon

Calista and I were hanging out at our onetime favorite bar--she was in town from Alabama--quality time, you know--killing buckets of Coronas--and hopefully wenching. We were playing pool with this couple, well, that's an assumption--pretty safe I suppose, guy, girl, whatever…

I was reconsidering the investment of four quarters in the game. Generally when we play partners I can relax a little--she being a certified shark, she usually carries me--but not tonight. Tonight, neither of us was dropping our shots worth a damn.

Cal was ending beer number nine and had somehow missed the window; that place where skill and relaxation converge? And you're playing like Fast Eddie Felson taking on the Fat Man? Well, it wasn't working. Cal was just flat, no English and way too much green. Meaning--we were in the process of losing yet another game.

I had to go to the drain room. You know how bad those places can be? I'll tell you--standing at the urinal, I tend to hold my breath for the whole time I'm in there, if it takes longer than one lung-full of air I only breathe through my mouth. Well the point is, I wasn't gone very long, but when I returned there was a nasty verbal ninja scene going down.

Cal and this Indian chick were nose to nose. That would be East Indian if you were keeping track. Seems the lady felt Cal had maligned her man. Cal had called him a dick cause he kept telling his partner how to shoot and she wasn't that bad a shot. So Cal got all offended--for her, the Indian chick I mean. The confrontation had gone from zero to thermonuclear in less time than it takes to poke your eye with a mascara wand. The girl started tossing the C word around and I got real nervous. I figured to break down my stick, get Cal in tow and hit the road--pronto. I grabbed my pal by the arm.

"Let it go. We're starting to collect an audience here…" I hissed.

Cookie Crumbles

"Back off RoRo, I'm gonna teach the bitch some manners."

"Bad idea, B-A-D bad idea. Remember that whole rule thing about avoiding the police? Remember calling me at 2 o'clock in the morning for bail? Remember being scared shitless? Huh? Do ya?" Without waiting for a response I continued. "Hey, today is Thursday. Karaoke night at Miss Kitty's Saloon…let's head over there. Didn't you get lucky last time we were there?"

"You know I did","" Cal said, poking me in the ribs. "The foxy China doll, yeah. OK, let's go."

Cal turned back to the table for a parting shot. "Hey Kavitha, you know what? You're pathetic. You and your Mr. Man deserve each other. I'm over trying to help you. Have a nice life."

As we headed for the door all I heard was sputtering, no whizzing pool cues, and I breathed a lot easier.

"Hey, how'd you know her name was Kavitha?" I asked as we got in the car.

"I don't, just so happens that some other princess whom I hate is named Kavitha."

"Oh," I said. Thinking, never get on her bad side.

Miss Kitty's, totally a blue-collar place in a town that's an ocean of Lexus and Beemers, was just a few hundred yards down the street. Its facade was decorated with cactus and wagon wheels and criss-cross faux timbers. A low ceiling kept heavy smoke hanging in the air waiting for a breeze that wasn't coming. My eyes started to sting as soon as we walked in.

We settled into a table half way down the bar. We were lucky--it was the only open space in the saloon. Guess Karaoke was still real popular with this crowd. We started singing "Leaving on a Jet Plane"--that's one of Cal's songs--but the guy on stage was singing "Devil in a Blue Dress". A man at the table next to us piped up. He was an older guy--older than me anyway--with a head of dark hair, going a little silver at the temples.

Cookie Crumbles

"Hey, why don't you guys write down that song title and turn it in to Doug. Then you can sing your little hearts out...UP THERE!"

Oof, only here thirty seconds and chastised already. "We're sorry, we didn't think anyone would care..."

"Hey, really no big deal...I'm just yanking your chain. I've never seen you two here before."

"Actually we were here once, a few months back. But we used to hang out up the street ALL the time. Played a lot of pool there."

"Oh yeah? I got kinda burnt out on that place, haven't been back since they changed the name," said our new friend.

"It's still pretty much the same." I said. "Ya knoooow--you sure look a lot like someone on TV. I can't quite fix on it..."

"You think?" he said, smiling broadly. "People tell me that all the time."

"Yeah! Martin Sheen! Mr. President, pleased to meet you..." I said sticking out my hand.

t's it," he replied, taking a little bow while he shook my hand even though he was sitting down. "Haven't figured out a way to make money off it. But it's probably too late since the show tanked."

"You're both crazy, I don't see it at all," said Cal.

Cal was busy scoping the possible hook-ups and coming up empty. It's a funny place. Definitely NOT a gay bar and yet, the last time we were here no one seemed to notice that Calista and that Asian chick were dancing so tight it was like they only had one pair of feet between them. Oh well, sometimes the game gets called on account of dark.

The DJ didn't have many singers in the rotation. It was less than an hour to closing. He called out Cal's name pretty quickly after I put up the request slip for her.

Calista was front and center singing her favorite number--Bob Segar's "Turn the Page". She interprets Segar like you wouldn't believe; she's got a real smoke and whisky voice. I was trying to get the lone bartender's attention. This fellow [wearing a purple sweatshirt in July, I thought that

Cookie Crumbles

was weird] sitting next to where I was standing was badmouthing the guy--saying how much better the bar ran when he was keeping it. He was about my height, I guess, not heavy not thin. Kinda average. Short neat hair, not unattractive.

I waved a twenty at the hustling barkeep to get some traction and…

"Dude, what's with those nails?" Mr. Purple Sweatshirt said.

My nails always grab people's attention. They're a half inch long and polished with clear coat. Utterly real, no acrylics.

I looked at him and quickly ran thru a number of responses. I decided on the truth.

"What do YOU think is with these nails?" I answered.

"Well I don't know, that's why I asked!"

"The truth is, I'm a drag queen."

"You are not."

"Yes--I am."

"No you're NOT," he said quite forcefully.

"YES--I am." I said as I fished my wallet out of my back pocket.

"You're not a queen. That's a picture of a real girl."

"Nope, the girl is me, " I said as I handed him the wallet-sized pic of me in a blue metallic dress and long curly hair performing at a suburban club.

"Wow, you're hot! Um, I mean…I mean I'm sure lot's of people tell you that what you do is cool and all but I'm kinda weirded out by it."

"OK, whatever," I started to move away. He stopped me.

"Um, do you like girls…or boys?"

I didn't answer, just held out my hand, palm up and then flipped it, back and forth, a few times. He got the message. He sorta made a gurgling noise and I decided to go back to my table. But as I left I lightly punched him on the shoulder, like straight guys do, ya know?

The night wore down to the last few songs and as the DJ called the last singer I noted that it was Mr. Purple Sweatshirt who made his way to the front of the room. I was bowled over when the familiar notes of the Kink's

Cookie Crumbles

"Lola" blasted out of the speakers. Obviously Mr. PS was sending me a message, but just what did it mean? He did a passable job singing. I swore he was looking only at me. As the last notes faded away, the bartender called out the traditional "Ya don't have to go home, but ya can't stay here" coda and brought up the house lights.

There is NOTHING more painful than being caught in the house lights with 12-hour-old makeup, then I remembered I was in boy drag, no sweat! Whew, that was cool. I looked around, said goodnight to Martin Sheen and tried to get Cal to finish her last Corona. I didn't see Mr. PS sitting back at the bar; he must have left right after his song.

"All right you homeless bums--ya got 7 minutes to haul ass outa here." The bartender seemed very sincere.

I could see a flashing red and blue Mars bar through the front window. The police had arrived to watch people practice DUI. Some folks had been making regular bar-lot-bar round trips the whole time we were there. They weren't in sight now. I wondered if the cops had busted them for weed or what?

"Cal, come on, drink up. Hey, sorry that Asian girl wasn't here tonight. You musta been kinda bored, huh?"

"It was OK, at least I got to sing three songs in forty-five minutes. That's well worth the trip from Alabama. Hey, what's with you and that guy?"

"Him? He's way weird. He says he doesn't like drag queens but then he goes and sings me that song! He disappeared right after."

"Well, I tell ya, he creeps me out, " Cal said.

Cal took forever to finish her beer. We were some of the very last people to leave the bar; meaning at least 15 or 20 minutes had passed since last call. The bartender said to come back soon, I think he meant it. As we cleared the doorway I saw Mr. PS loitering on the sidewalk.

"Hey dude!"

"Um--hi. I really don't go by 'dude'. Friends call me RoRo. I thought

Cookie Crumbles

you'd left..."

"Did you like your song?"

"Sure. Always been a big Kinks fan. Thanks."

"RoRo, I'm hungry and tired. Let's go," Cal said.

"I'll meet you at the car," I said and tossed her the keys.

She snatched them out of the air and was gone.

"So--what's the deal, ah..."

"Ross"

"Uh huh."

The silence hung there between us. He wasn't really my type. He became intensely interested in the sidewalk. I wasn't going to start.

"You coming back next time?" he asked.

"You mean for Karaoke?"

"Yeah..."

"Doubtful, my girlfriend is the Karaoke queen, and she'll be back in Alabama."

"Oh. But you live up here?"

"Yup, right past downtown."

I wasn't sure how I wanted to handle this guy, so I let the air quiet down. We were saved from further awkwardness by the arrival of some friend of Ross'.

"Hey man, let's get going! There's a burrito big as my head with my name on it down at Killer Burrito. Bar crowd's gonna fill the joint up soon. Let's go, let's go!"

"All right, I'm coming," said Ross.

He looked at me, expectantly. I suddenly felt really bad, acting all superior and shit, so I said, "Hey man, see ya around, OK?"

He smiled, warmly, and walked off briskly with his friend. I thought, maybe he was cool, just really repressed? By the time I got back to my car, Cal was passed out in the passenger seat and the doors--were locked...

Cookie Crumbles

One Night In Red

It was way late, and it was cold. The air was heavy with water somewhere between a mist and a drizzle. Jim and I were on our way to Foxy's for one more drink before heading home. We were both leathered up--"motorcycle drag," we laughed. It was fashionable, you walk into any gay bar and the smell of old leather just smacks ya.

It was so late that there were open tables along the outside wall facing the bar. We settled into one and debated what to have.

I snagged the bill out of Jim's hand and started away from the table. As I crossed Foxy's main room to the long bar I spied a tall lanky girl at the rail. Her deep auburn hair hung down to the right obscuring her face as I approached. She was wearing an old motorcycle jacket, so worn that the creases were silver white. I could see an AC/DC t-shirt tucked into a leather micro-mini. Big chunky boots added at least another two inches to her height.

As I leaned over the bar waving my--actually, Jim's--money to get the bartender's attention, she turned towards me, flipped her tresses up, and repositioned her sunglasses atop her head, keeping her flame hair out of her eyes for a few seconds. She was stunning, a classic beauty wearing only powder, mascara, and lipstick and not really much of that.

The barman strolled over. I ordered a Black Russian and a Rolling Rock for the trip back to the table. I was doing my best not to stare--and failing. She, however, was staring at me, quite openly. And then she spoke, and I was awash in two streams of thought. The first was that this fabulous creature of the night was addressing me as if I was someone she already knew.

"Hey, it's you," she said.

"Um, hi," I said.

"I just wanted to say I'm sorry, apologize I guess, for the way I treated you the other night at Denny's," she said.

Cookie Crumbles

The second stream was the sudden--sudden as a green stick fracture--realization that this outrageously beautiful woman was a guy. I've been around the block, I've seen a million drag shows, but until she spoke, there was not the slightest hint in my mind that she was anything other than what she appeared to be. And I was seriously hard.

"You don't owe me an apology," I said, grasping for words.

"Well thanks," she said.

"You're welcome."

"Let's go back to your table."

"Okay," I said, reeling. This doesn't happen to me very often.

"Tony," she said to the bartender, "get me a Tangueray and tonic."

Jim was watching with a bemused smile on his face as we came to the table. I'm sure I looked like I just won the lottery, shit-eating grin and all.

"This is Jim," I said.

"Hi...Cordelia," she said extending her hand.

"Are you two a couple?" she asked.

"Nope, just friends," I answered.

"Well, good, then I'm sure Jim won't mind leaving us alone, would you Jim?"

I was stunned. I had never seen anyone act so, so, in charge. Jim was one of my dearest friends, and I should have reacted to her effrontery by telling her that her demand was ludicrous--worse, offensive. But I didn't; I just gave Jim a look. A look that said, "get the fuck outta here." I felt craven, but excited, like I had just crested the highest peak of a really wicked old wooden coaster, and that long crazy whoosh was staring me in the face.

"Oh, not at all, not at all. Have a good time kids. I'll see ya later," said Jim.

"Okay," I said timidly, watching Jim leave.

I looked at her, expectantly.

Cookie Crumbles

"So, I've only been back in the mid-dash-west for a few weeks, and I'm bored shitless already," she said.

"Back?"

"Yeah, I grew up here. Ran away to New York when I was seventeen."

"Why'd ya come back?"

"Why does anyone come home after making a whole new life? A million reasons."

"Tell me a few-- I got all night."

She laughed as she took her glasses off her head, shook her hair for effect, and replaced the glasses as a headband. I got the feeling that as far as restraint goes, the sunglasses were as far as she went.

"You're funny," she said. "You remind me of my husband."

"Husband?"

"Yeah, deceased. His name was Joey. He was the love of my life. He had the 'body of life'--like a god, no, not like, he was a god. So beautiful, I still can't believe he's dead. But he wouldn't stop, couldn't stop, ever. He had to have too much--of everything. Like they say: sex, drugs and rock-n-roll. He was in a race to see what would kill him first. Drugs won."

"I'm sorry."

"Are you? Then get me another drink, Tan…"

"I know, Tangueray and Tonic," I said as I moved for the bar.

I half expected her to be gone when I got back, but she was still there.

"One T-n-T for the lady," I said, handing over her drink.

"Thanks," she said. "You got a car?"

"Yeah."

"Let's go," she said as she picked up her almost full drink. It was really funny, getting in a car with a mixed drink came close to freaking me out, but the cigarette case in my jacket pocket with five joints didn't bother me at all. Life is weird.

I had primo parking just two meters west on Belmont. I had to open

Cookie Crumbles

her door--I never locked the car anymore since someone had used a log to open the window and steal my radio one night up at the BistroToo--seeing as her hands were full with her purse and her drink and her cigarette. As I slid in on the driver's side, she set her drink up on the dash and relit her smoke. She leaned a bit across the console. Damn buckets, I thought to myself. I hadn't turned the ignition yet, and the windows quickly turned opaque. We chatted, in a strange blend of comfortable strangers and intimate friends.

"So, what did you do in New York?"

"Drugs, men, modeling--in that order. I had to leave, get away from the smack. Lost a lot of jobs to that shit. Show up late, or not at all, once too many times and you're history. Manhattan is a very small town. Everybody knows your business. So, I'm over that, totally."

"Really?"

"Sure--well, I do a little coke now and then, just to be sociable…and Xanax, but that's 'script, so doesn't count."

"Oh," I said. "So you modeled?"

She cocked a perfectly shaped eyebrow so high it grazed my moon roof.

"You're fishing. You know Scavulo?"

"Of course."

"You do have libraries in the mid-dash-west, take a look at his last coffee table collection. I'm in it. Satisfy yourself," she said coldly.

"Sor…ry, you're awful touchy aren't you?"

"I'm not! I'm just so tired of people and how they think--'she uses drugs, you can't trust her, she lies all the time.' I'll tell you when I'm fucking lying, all right?"

She looked very upset. It was obvious that her moods were majorly mercurial.

"The thing is, I'd like to get clean. Really, but I need help. I can't do rehab. I tried that in New York. I need a … someone, like a coach.

Cookie Crumbles

Someone I can talk to. Would you help me?"

"Cordelia, you're asking a lot, something I'm not sure I could commit to. Are you even sober now? Will you remember this conversation tomorrow?"

"I know, I understand what you're thinking. You're thinking I'm some psycho-bitch, some kinda psychic vampire, that's okay--forget I said anything at all."

She took a long drag on her cigarette and then a quick sip on her T-n-T. I kinda wished she'd just slam it. She put the drink back on the dash. I reached out to her, she leaned forward and we embraced. Our lips tentatively found each other. It was a sweet kiss.

"I can't promise to be there for you all the time. But I really want to help you, I do. Let's at least start by being friends. Can we do that?"

She leaned in again and kissed me. I was having an out-of-body experience. I literally felt like I was watching Cordelia and myself play out this little drama while floating above it. A beautiful woman with that delicious little extra treat, right here in my arms, a long held fantasy of mine come to life. I was coming up on delirious. She took my left hand, raised it to her lips and kissed my palm. She pulled up her t-shirt and used my hand to cup her right breast. It was small but all natural, warm and perfect.

I leaned over the console and put my mouth over her breast and circled her nipple with my tongue. It quickly hardened and grew substantially. Cordelia's fingers threaded through my hair, and she let a little moan escape her throat. I slipped my free hand under her skirt only to encounter her rather impervious tights. I couldn't find the slightest hint of her slowpoke. That really annoyed me, almost as much as the bucket seats. I momentarily abandoned her breast to return to her lips while she slid partway up the seatback to raise her butt off the seat and get her tights pulled down. Finally, sweet success was had, down to just her panties.

Cookie Crumbles

"You know what?" she asked, stopping my reach.

"What?"

"I fucked this guy once--a pretty big star in industrial music, always wore those huge hats. I can't remember his name--ya know who I mean?"

"Ah, I...wait a minute, yeah, Hal, Hal...something."

"Right, anyway I ran into him outside the Chelsea late one night after he'd played at the Limelight. We got to talking, and he invited me up to his room. I'll never forget this, he was so sweet. I mean, I just jumped him as soon as we hit the couch. He was hard quick, and he exploded--I mean tons. He sat back and grinned, told me that I was one fantastic cocksucker, and then he reached out and pushed my skirt up. I asked him what the fuck he thought he was doing, and he said one good turn deserved another. He told me I was a beautiful girl, and that he didn't care what I had in my panties. He said that if I had a pussy he'd eat it, and if I had a dick he'd suck it."

"Well," I said, "I'm hoping it's meat and not fish. Not that there's anything wrong with seafood."

She laughed as I pulled her panties down and then all hell broke loose. Somehow in all the repositioning I'd done I had hit my four-way flashers. A squad had rolled up, and its flood was pouring about a million foot-candles through the fogged up windows. I heard a metallic rapping on the passenger side glass. Cordelia rolled it down. The rapping had been from a standard police issue flashlight, and its business end was now sweeping the interior of my car. I swore softly as the light illuminated the squat glass of gin from Foxy's. This was going to be an unpleasant interlude.

"You might want to pull up your panties, missy," said the cop as he took in the scene.   Working the graveyard in Boystown is not a premium assignment. I was hoping he was cool with alternative types.

He hadn't asked for IDs yet. He stretched out a hand and picked the glass off the dash, ran it under his nose and replaced it.

Cookie Crumbles

"Well, exactly what do we have here?" he asked.

I had no idea what to say. But I figured that if we were going to talk our way out of it, it had to get done before another squad showed up.

"Officer, my friend and I were just talking…"

"Talking? Looked a little more than just talking to me."

"It does look that way, I have to admit but really, nothing…" I said.

"Listen, you two, I probably got better things to do than roust a couple of sex addicts, but don't be shining me on, you get it? Now, why don't we start with your names, and why, exactly, you have open liquor in your car?"

"Um, yeah, sure. My name is Les, ah Nuenn, as for the liquor, it it…"

Cordelia hadn't said a single word since the tap-tap-tapping at the window began. She appeared to have a slight smile playing on her face. That bothered me. I felt more than a little crazed. For some really strange reason it was important to me not to look as panicked as I felt--not in front of Cordelia.

"The booze is mine Officer. He told me not to bring it, and I just didn't listen. I don't listen well at all. I'm sorry…"

"I see…I guess…if it was an empty glass it wouldn't be much of an issue," he said.

Cordelia snatched it off the dash, drained it, and dropped it in her shoulder bag.

The cop just rolled his eyes and tried to suppress a smile.

"So, missy, you've managed not to identify yourself as yet, what is your name?"

"Cordelia Carson"

"Carson, eh?" he said, "I don't suppose you have any actual ID?"

"Well, I don't have a car, so no driver's license, never got any official ID, no, I guess not.

"Well, it's against my better judgment--okay, listen, I'll cut you two a break this time, but the next time you feel the need to play slap and tickle,

Cookie Crumbles

take it home. Got me?"

"Yes, sir--remember that Les! Next time you won't be so lucky." Cordelia said.

"Um, right." I said.

"All right then, get moving," he said.

The officer was quickly back in his squad and rolling off.

"He didn't seem all that interested in running us through the cop shop."

"Lucky for us," I said. "It's been quite an evening, but I need to get my ass back to the 'burbs. Where do you live? I'll drop you off."

"You're bailing on me? I could make you breakfast."

"Can I get a rain check?"

"Hhhmmmn, sure. Orchard, off Diversy."

It was a very short drive.

"Tell me when to stop," I said as we came up behind the Century Mall.

"Right here."

We stopped in front of a four-story walkup, not too dilapidated. Cordelia leaned over and kissed me hard on the lips, and then she scampered out of the car before I could ask for her number. As she passed my window she motioned to roll it down and tossed a scrunched up cocktail napkin at me. She didn't wait to see if I caught it, but turned on her heel and quickly walked to her building and let herself in. She was gone as if she'd turned to smoke.

What a night. Pulling onto the expressway, heading west with the pink light of dawn spreading in my rearview mirror, I felt like I'd dodged a bullet. I could just as easily have ended up in jail this morning instead of heading off back to suburbia.

I felt an incredible edge of attraction for her--sexual tension, adventure, danger, however you want to define it. Her napkin was still in my right fist, still clenched, I realized as I drove on. I opened the napkin and found her number framed in a lipsticked kiss.

Cookie Crumbles

Cookie Crumbles

The Night of Two Sami's

Calista, Ginger, MaryAnn and RoRo were in fine Mardi Gras form. MaryAnn was the virgin this trip, you could tell because she was wearing boots with four inch heels, chunky, but four inches none the less. Ginger wasn't even in drag, black leather short shorts; a black wifebeater and glory stomper boots completed her look, so she wasn't quite out of drag. Calista was wearing her favorite Mardi Gras colored striped polo shirt over skintight blue jeans, sneakers and no bra. She was ready to earn her beads. And RoRo? Wearing a red tank dress and leopard print shrug--with a pushup bra that made her boy boobs as prominent as a Catholic girl on vacation in Cancun. As a veteran she was wearing sling back low-heeled wedgies.

The gang's sartorial splendor on parade had started out on a deep ocean blue perfect day for the Queens judging on St Anne's street at noon. It was successful to the tune of a half-dozen Walgreen's throwaway cameras. Unfortunately another well-partied Lundi Gras over the previous night had precluded getting to Canal Street in time for the Zulu parade yet again, but the consensus, just like the Cubbies, was--wait till next year.

Mardi Gras day eventually bled off into Mardi Gras evening. Buckets of Bloody Marys and Hurricanes had been tossed back in gay bars, straight bars, alleys and patios; their trek through the Quarter--if mapped--would look like a spastic black mamba tying itself in knots.

Tradition demanded a visit to Cal's Doorway [so named on Cal's first trip to the Crescent City way way back in '93--ten years earlier], a painted shut French door slightly to the left of the regular entrance of the Golden Star on Decatur. MaryAnn had not been on that trip, so as they walked up the street to the restaurant RoRo and Ginger began to fill MaryAnn in on whence the name had come.

"I'm going to tell you EXACTLY how it happened." Said Ginger.

"Don't believe a word these bitches say!" Said Cal.

Cookie Crumbles

"Oh like you have any surviving memory of it at all," said RoRo, laughing.

Ginger continued, "After drinking a vat of Hurricanes we had stopped by chance at the Golden Star. We decided it was dinnertime. Cal could barely hold her head above the table. When the waiter queried her for her order she had a one-word answer."

✤✤✤✤✤

"FISH!" Calista bellowed at the waiter.

Shortly a platter of blackened catfish was set down in front of her and after a mouthful or two of heavy Cajun spiced fish dripping tartar sauce-- she made a slow-motion dash to the sidewalk, which, in itself, was very amusing. Cal threw herself into a trash barrel nearly as tall as she was and rocketed Hurricane mix at near light speed.

The table burst into riotous laughter. After all, excess is the baseline for Mardi Gras.

"I told her to slow down after she drained her second drink before I had even finished my first." Said RoRo, who then left the table and went out to see if there was anything she should do.

Standing behind Cal, RoRo said "Jeez girl, until I realized that all that red stuff was Hurricane juice I thought you were bleeding to death! Damn. Clean your face! You going to come back in and finish eating?"

Calista was feeling around for the sidewalk with her right foot. Both her boobs were still inside the barrel. And her legs just weren't long enough.

"Ah, not today...I'm just gonna..." she released her deathgrip on the barrel and slid down the side until she approximated standing. She crab-walked across the broken pavement to the previously mentioned painted shut French door next to the entrance of the Golden Star. "I...I'm just gonna scooch down here in the doorway for a minute, OK?" She said as she stretched out.

Cookie Crumbles

RoRo said, "OK…" and returned to the table. The troop was hungry and cleaned their plates to a mother's satisfaction. Twilight is short; the night comes quickly in the Quarter. Ginger was the first to notice the flashing blue light."

"Uh oh, unless this is the K-Mart cafeteria we got trouble." Said Ginger.

Cal's limp body was plainly visible thru the glass panels of the door and now a female cop stood over the semi-conscious girl.

"Wake up sister, you can't sleep on the street in New Orleans. Not even during Mardi Gras." The officer extended a boot and gently nudged Cal's arm. "Come on--talk to me or I'm calling a wagon…you don't want to come to in the lockup looking as pretty as you do."

The cop was gentle; she wasn't being a hard-ass at all.

"Oh that's OK. I'm just going to sleep here for a minute. I'm fine." Calista was totally oblivious to the fact that she was not making things better.

"Ah no, it's not OK miss. You've got to get up or I'm going to have to take you in."

"No no really, I'll just sleep here for a minute."

"I'm sorry Officer, she's with us. She can be as obstinate as a fifty-dollar car on a January morning in Chicago. We'll get a cab and take her back to our B&B." Ginger said. She had quickly moved out to the sidewalk after noticing the interview going bad.

RoRo spied an empty cab coming down Decatur and flagged it to a stop. Ginger opened the passenger door and went back for Cal. The cop actually helped motivate her into the taxi.

"Thanks girls," said the cop. "I'm off in 20 and I sure didn't want to do any extra paperwork tonight. My girlfriend is probably collecting way too many beads as it is and I need to catch up with her."

She waved from her squad as she rolled off to the big party that was still building to a full bore, all stops out, patented, Big Easy--see you at dawn at the Café Du Monde--kind of blowout.

Cookie Crumbles

Our trio had piled into their taxi and was about to speed away…

"Hey y'all, don't forget her fish, I boxed it up for ya!" said the waiter waving a bag from the doorway.

✦✦✦✦✦

"And that is the reason this is "Cal's Doorway". Said Ginger--relating the end of that afternoon ten years earlier.

"A fine bunch of friends you are! I thought our rule is anything that happens at Mardi Gras STAYS at Mardi Gras!" Exclaimed Calista.

"Well, look around Honey--we're AT Mardi Gras, no violation of protocol here!" Said Ginger.

The Gang of Four caught a cab back to the Garden District for a disco nap at the painted lady they called home every Carnival season in New Orleans. This year the weather and the Bush recession had conspired to keep attendance way down. Of course, the benefit of that poor showing was that there were no lines of hungry patrons waiting to get in to the better restaurants and--if you were lucky enough to get a cab--you were actually able to get to Lee's Circle from the Quarter for only seven bucks!

So the four settled in for a little snore. It was only 9 PM and the strippers wouldn't get into gear until 11 at least.

"OK, everyone has their alarm set, right? I swear if we wake up at 3 o'clock in the morning again like last time I will have someone's balls on my key chain." Ginger said sweetly.

"Well if you ask real nice you can just have mine, I'm done with 'em." Said RoRo.

"Worry about getting your own sorry ass up and leave the rest of us out of it." Said Cal.

MaryAnn was already asleep.

10 PM was marked by a jangle of alarms--all were up and active, jockeying for position at the one and only full-length mirror in the house.

Cookie Crumbles

"Can someone carry my cigarettes in their purse?" Asked Cal. "That mutant at the convenience store gave me a soft pack instead of the box and I didn't notice it till we were gone half way down the block. I can only get my license and lighter into the back pocket of these jeans."

"No problem honey," said RoRo, catching the pack in mid-air as Cal tossed it across the room.

"Hey RoRo, I keep forgetting to ask you, how did that ass thing end up?" said Calista.

"Oh--you mean Jake? He decided he was straight, living with some skank he met at GA."

"No dipshit, I'm talking about your personal ass, the extra big one hanging off your tailbone." She said laughing.

"OK. Well, are you sure you want to hear about it? It's really gross…"

"Just gimme the highlights."

"Turns out I had congenital anal pockets. They were infected, oozing, the surgeon cut 'em out, once I heal I can return to a life of sleaze." RoRo continued.

"How long?"

"A few more weeks."

"Ummm you know I'm totally entranced by this scintillating Discovery Channel seminar--but if everyone is ready?" asked Ginger.

"OK…OK--I get the message--let's go, while MaryAnn is still young and pretty," said RoRo.

Cal and MaryAnn gave their assent and back out into the night's embrace they went. Luckily they caught a cab right on the corner at Prytania and were soon zooming towards Vieux Carre'. While zooming is generally a good thing, a cab driver watching Jay Leno while zooming can be, ahhh, scary. The TV was definitely after market, with a coat hanger instead of an antenna and was mounted somewhat below the dash where a front seat passenger would have her knees, so RoRo took the front, cause she is a short girl. It quickly dawned on Ginger that this was a gypsy

Cookie Crumbles

cab as the meter had gone missing.

"Ah, sir...I...I don't see your name."

"Alfie."

"Well Alfie, how much to Canal Street?"

"Twelve bucks--and that's a bargain--it being Mardi Gras night. That's my special pretty girls and boy rate."

"OK, Alfie. Sounds good to us."

Amazingly, even with Alfie watching the Tonight Show instead of the road, the trip was completed successfully. As Alfie pulled over to let them out, RoRo volunteered to pay the fare. She counted out twelve dollars and then added a five for a tip, since it was Mardi Gras and she was feeling generous!

Alfie held up the five and said "You can keep the tip if you kiss me."

"Tongue?" Said RoRo.

"Of course."

RoRo leaned in, parted her full red lips, connected open-mouthed and made a quick roundabout of Alfie's tongue with her own--ending with a big theatrical smack.

"Happy Mardi Gras honey" She said as she plucked the proffered five and exited the cab.

Crossing Canal Street while a parade is going on can be dicey--sometimes the cops are less forgiving than other times. This night though the parade had ground to a halt somewhere up Canal and after a bit of a wait, a large gap had appeared where the trolley cars turn up from St Charles. People had begun slipping around the barricades and crossing the Neutral Ground to the Quarter, as did our girls.

While the majority of gay bars are in the gay section of the Quarter, some, like the Corner Pocket where the quartet was headed, are on the straight side. Once in the Quarter they walked up Iberville past the beginning of Bourbon looking for the cross street that takes them to the stripper bar. Someone they had met at lunch had recommended the

Cookie Crumbles

`Pocket for the quality of it's strip show. Stripping in New Orleans had taken a huge dive ever since the Mississippi River Bottom had gone away from being a show bar.

As they passed a three-step stoop with a wrought iron railing at the front of a pink shotgun house with traditional white shutters, a man with a cigarette hanging from his mouth standing in the doorway called out to them.

"Hey, any of y'all got a light?"

"Sure, sugar, I know I do."

RoRo dug into her purse looking to find her Harley-Davidson lighter, she loved igniting the cigarette of whomever she was chatting up with such a macho device, it was always good for ten minutes of conversation including her favorite story about the guy that worked the assembly line in Milwaukee who stole a Sportster piece by piece in his lunch box.

"Here ya go honey." Said RoRo as she lit the man's very retro unfiltered Lucky Strike.

"Thanks…You got a bit of La Liz going on with that hair and those eyes, don't 'cha girl?"

"Well, I have been told that from time to time…" She said, patting the back of her hair into place in case any single strand had broken the bonds of high gravity hair spray and moved a millimeter out of place.

"Hold on a minute, I've got some beads for ya."

He came back and handed RoRo a few loops of shiny gold beads.

"Thank you Darling, you're a treasure." Said RoRo.

"Do you have any beads for me?" Said Calista, feeling left out.

"I don't mind earning them." She said grabbing the bottom of her shirt with both hands.

"Sorry honey, no offense, but if I want milk, I just go to the store. But here, take a few of these; if you're a friend of Liz, you're a friend of mine. Have a good night. Stay outa trouble! And Liz, you ever lonely you know where to find me."

Cookie Crumbles

"OK, I'll remember that. You're a sweet sweet man and I really appreciate the lovely thought." Said RoRo.

"Jeez, how come no one wants to give me any beads?" Asked MaryAnn.

"Don't worry your pretty little head, people haven't even started trying to get in your pants yet, it's early, give them time." Said Ginger.

A few short blocks later they came up on the Corner Pocket. The windows on either side of the front door were plastered with small posters advising that in celebration of Mardi Gras a troupe of dancers had been imported all the way from Montreal. No mention of how the local dancers felt about it.

There was another sign that stated that cameras were strictly forbidden. This was the result of Christian troublemakers who had videotaped parties during the previous Southern Decadence celebration and triumphantly screened them for the bubbas in Baton Rouge. In New Orleans money talks and bullshit walks but the state pols still needed to be seen on TV condemning the damn filthy queers in the Quarter.

There was nowhere to sit at the bar once they paid the cover and entered. Quite a few people were standing about waiting for the strippers to take the stage. Stage being a slight misnomer, it was a ? inch slab of plywood laid atop the regulation tavern sized pool table. Cal and RoRo perched their butts on the stage. RoRo was more careful than Cal as she didn't want to run her pantyhose with a stray splinter from the rough-cut board. Ginger went to get drinks and MaryAnn was in search of a rest room.

By the time the girls were on their second round of drinks the dancing boys had begun their rotation. The four friends stood in front of the stage, but off to one side so not to block the view from the bar. The first two dancers had been very thin, one blonde, one auburn haired and neither had attracted a lot of tips from the crowd while they were on stage.

The rules about how much attention one can pay to a stripper's cock after stuffing their g-string with cash vary wildly based on the city, the bar

Cookie Crumbles

and the dancer. Generally it's OK to hold it, stroke it, maybe even kiss it and in rare circumstances, briefly suck it. The two boys who had come off the stage were working the room, flirting and showing their wares; generally pumping up their cash flow.

The next dancer was absolutely stunning. He was not big, but he was perfect. Maybe 5'8", 145 pounds of beautifully defined but completely fluid muscle. Thick short black hair, but longer than a buzz cut, covered his shapely skull. And he could really dance, very gracefully. He eschewed any costume, wearing a tank top and loose shorts, both black and a pair of lace up boots. His skin was unmarked by scars or tattoos and was quite dark but he possessed European features.

He was a crowd favorite and by the time he stripped down to his g-string a line five deep was waiting to tip him. MaryAnn said she favored the skinny blonde that had taken the stage first but the other three all dug singles out of their pockets or purses and got in line.

The dancer was friendly and attentive to all, but especially to Calista. When she came up to the stage he flashed her a big white perfectly maintained smile. She was tentative as she held out her dollar. He pulled his g-string out so she could drop the dollar in. She never touched him, but plainly saw his semi-erect cock. She giggled and spun away.

"Damn it, he's straight. I hate that." Ginger said.

"Don't be so sure." Said RoRo.

RoRo had five singles in hand and tucked two into the dancer's g-string above his ass, two in front and took her time wrapping the last one around his--by now--fairly stiff dick. She gave it a good squeeze and he didn't pull away--in fact he leaned in and brushed his lips across RoRo's cheek. Ginger took her place and RoRo stood next to Calista and encouraged her to get a little more rowdy with another handful of singles.

"Oh--you're back." Said the dancer to Calista.

"Yeah, my friends said I was acting way too shy, and that's so really not me. I'm usually quite assertive." She said as she did her very first US

Cookie Crumbles

currency cock wrap, with a double squeeze. The boy had squatted with his ass only a scant inch above the plywood to give her better access and also brought them both to eye level. His eyes registered the squeezes.

"What's your name?" He asked.

"Calista."

"What's yours?"

"Sami."

With that he sprang to his feet and returned to his routine. Calista wandered back to RoRo and Ginger. MaryAnn was still missing in action.

When Sami finished his set he left the stage and went to the dressing room. Shortly he returned and instead of working the room he came over to Calista, RoRo and Ginger.

"Hi. Calista is a very unusual name, but something tells me it suits you. In fact I don't think I've ever met another person named Calista." Said Sami.

"Oh I've been told that before, I do try to live up to it, I like to leave people with a good impression."

"You have an excellent start on that." Sami said.

While Sami was focused on Calista, Ginger was rubbing his ass and RoRo was pushing an occasional dollar bill into his thong. The dancer seemed able to multi-task nicely as he leaned back into Ginger's ministering hands and continued to chat with Cal and still flashed RoRo a smile with every deposit.

The conversation seemed to be getting past initial pleasantries when an older gentleman with silver hair wearing a European style suit came up and spoke a few sentences to Sami in French.

"Oui" He said to the man.

"Henri has reminded me that I need to be more generous with the rest of my audience. Don't go away, I'll be back." He said--more to Calista than anyone else.

The next dancer took the stage but he did not hold any interest for the gang. RoRo volunteered to get refills. The service island at the near end of

Cookie Crumbles

the bar was four deep so she walked the perimeter of the oval bar looking for another island. Not finding one she just wedged her way into the bar waving her cash.

Sami returned shortly after RoRo had come back with the drinks, tequila for herself and a Corona for Calista.

"Sami, can I get you a drink?" Asked RoRo.

"Sure, I'll have what you're having."

"One tequila coming up." Said RoRo pivoting on her heels.

"So what is it like living in Montreal?" Asked Calista.

"A lot like here, both have a strong French character, great food, fantastic night life…but Montreal is bitterly cold much of the year. So the subways are excellent."

"Really? Well, I'm from Chicago, we have all that--but without the French of course. Which is funny seeing as how Chicago was founded by a Black French guy."

"Yeah, I know, DuSable, right?"

"Yes, how did you know that?" Asked Cal.

"What, you think that because I strip for a living that I'm uneducated?"

"No! Of course not, most people from Chicago don't even know it, so I'm thinking, why would someone from Montreal? That's all, don't be offended."

"OK, just so you know--I'm a University student. Majoring in International Relations. I speak five languages."

"Well, you do look awfully smart." Said Cal laughing and squeezing Sami's penis. "I bet you wear those big black frame nerd glasses, don't you?"

"Only in class, I want my professors to know I'm serious."

"How long before you graduate?"

"Two more semesters."

"Where will you work?" Asked Cal.

"I expect I'll go to work for the government, in Ottawa."

Cookie Crumbles

"Really? Even with this…business…in your background?"

"Oh, I don't use my real name and I never do publicity shots that show my face." Said Sami.

The two continued to chat about all sorts of daily mundane life events until RoRo finally showed up with Sami's tequila.

"Sorry it took so long." Apologized RoRo. "No where near enough bartenders here.

Meanwhile MaryAnn was primping in the mirror of the Ladies room adding yet another layer of mascara to her already gorgeous eyes when two women walked in arms entwined. One was blonde with a very short do and the other had reddish hair trending toward purple in a long bob.

"Don't mind us dear, we're still in that disgusting kissy-face stage, we'll be over it soon."

"Oh don't worry, I think it's sweet, falling in love is wonderful." Said MaryAnn.

"Listen Linda," said the girl with the short do, "I don't need to watch you pee, really, so you'll have to let go." She was smiling broadly.

"OK Laura, but you wait right there with the pretty lady till I get out." Said Linda.

"But how do you know I'm going to wait here another second?" Asked MaryAnn.

"Because we're practically the only other women in the whole place and I'm sure you're desperate for female conversation by now, even if you've only been here five minutes." Said Linda as she shut the stall door.

MaryAnn realized that the two women had no clue that she was a boy. She was elated.

"So what are you ladies doing at a strip club anyway?" Asked MaryAnn.

"Well, my brother is one of the bartenders and we get to drink free all night." Said Laura.

"Oh then it makes sense." Said MaryAnn.

"How 'bout you?"

Cookie Crumbles

"I'm with friends, bar hopping, you know, it's my first Mardi Gras, I wanna see everything."

The flushing covered the sound of the stall door opening and Linda stepped out and went to the sink. After drying her hands she pulled her lipstick out and ran it across her lips.

"Thanks for keeping my girl company," Linda said, "Can I buy you a drink?"

"Sure."

MaryAnn found herself on the opposite side of the bar from her friends. She didn't mind--she was enjoying being a "real" girl with her new girlfriends, for a while at least.

Seeing she was with Linda and Laura the bartender quickly brought MaryAnn the Rum and Coke she requested, even though the drink was free she still left him a dollar tip.

"Thanks." MaryAnn said to the girls.

"Happy Mardi Gras." They said as they all clinked their glasses.

"So honey, where are you from?" Asked Laura.

"Chicago."

"And your friends too?"

"Yup, and where are you two from?"

"We're local girls, Metairie, one suburb up the road, this is our millionth Mardi Gras." Said Laura.

"I thought all the natives left town for Mardi Gras."

"Nah, just the straight ones, why would queers leave a party?" Said Linda laughing.

The skinny blonde stripper that had taken the stage first was still working the crowd and his bikini was finally looking stuffed with cash. He walked up to MaryAnn.

"Hey girl, I thought you were going to meet me by the john? Did you forget about me?"

"Umm no, not really, just sidetracked…" MaryAnn said, "Linda, Laura, this is Jesse."

Everyone said a polite hello.

"I just came off rotation, so if you're still interested, come to the dressing room." Said Jesse.

"OK, I'll see you there." Said MaryAnn.

"Color me confused," Said Laura, "You're straight? As in you like men?"

MaryAnn started laughing, and couldn't stop; finally she caught her breath.

"Actually I like men very much, but I'm so not straight…I'm a boy. Sorry."

The girls exchanged looks that were indicative of total mindfuck.

"I can't believe it, I have never met a boy as fem as you!" Said Linda.

"I don't believe it…" Said Laura as she ran her hand up MaryAnn's leg under her skirt until she squealed when she found MaryAnn's untucked penis.

"Now I'm the one that's sorry…" She said.

MaryAnn giggled, "No problem girls, listen, pretend your next drink is on me, OK? I've got to go find that skinny little outlaw. And thanks for making my day!"

+++++

Calista slipped her arms around Sami's neck and pulled his head towards her. She puckered her full caramel lips, opened her mouth and her curled tongue reached out for her playmate, but Sami jerked his head away and her lips spent themselves against his cheek.

"Hey, I said NO kissing!"

"I thought you were kidding." Cal answered. "That makes no sense, I've been playing with your cock and balls for the last half-hour--but you won't kiss me?"

"That's just business, my kisses are for love and they're not for sale."

Cookie Crumbles

Calista stood silent a moment as Sami's words ricocheted in her head. Her eyes telegraphed a serious message of "How dare you?" and her right hand left a red stinging imprint on Sami's face. Calista has a volcanic temper; fast running lava is only slightly hotter than her when she feels she's been wronged.

"You bastard!" She spit out as she spun and walked quickly away.

Sami simply rubbed his face and didn't look back as he returned to the dressing room.

The Euro-sharpdressed man said "What the fuck?"

Sami shrugged with Gallic indifference saying, "Women are too difficult, mais oui?"

With that the silvermaned man lifted Sami's face with a finger under his chin and leaned in for a very passion filled kiss…

MaryAnn left Jesse in the men's room just in time to see Calista exit the bar, she collected RoRo and Ginger and they ran as fast as their heels would allow to catch up with their seriously angry friend.

"Damn" said Calista "He was playing me, that little prick!"

"Welcome to life as a gay man honey." Said Ginger laughing uproariously.

"If it's any consolation, the boys in the bathroom said he's not even slightly bi and probably couldn't even have stayed hard long enough to get you off--unless he used his tongue…" said MaryAnn.

"You say that like it's a bad thing" Said Cal smiling--already starting to cool down.

"Well I guess we're done with the 'Pocket for the rest of this trip." Said RoRo. "Your picture will probably go up on the wall with a slash thru it."

Ginger suggested that they hit Good Friends, another reliable establishment for serious Mardi Gras partying and it was real close by.

+++++

Cookie Crumbles

The first floor of Good Friends was jammed end to end with men in various stages of fun and more serious Dionysian revels. The service islands of the bar were three deep and Cal and company were too thirsty for that. They shouldered their way to the staircase leading to the upper floor; the balcony always provided good people watching opportunities not to mention deep quiet shadows.

"Oooh look at that guy in the harness and leather collar." Said Cal as they left the landing. "He's so buff, I wonder if he likes girls?"

"I am so sure, don't you see the flashing pink neon sign above his head?" Ginger asked.

Cal walked over to the leather boy with a saucy--I don't care if I am in a gay bar--bounce and calmly pulled her Mardi Gras striped shirt up to her chin. The leather boy leaned over and bit down on her left nipple and pulled it back to him, stretching out her full round breast into a ice cream cone shape.

"Ouch!" Yelped Cal.

The leather boy was wearing chaps over nothing, well a sock really and MaryAnn grabbed a double handful of bubble butt and started rubbing while Cal leaned into an open mouthed kiss after the boy relinquished her breast. MaryAnn's skirt showed that she had definitely not tucked before leaving the house. RoRo was regretting she had used all the cameras on the Queens in the afternoon at the judging.

Ginger went out to the balcony and caught some cool night air. RoRo sat at the bar next to a handsome man with a ton of medallions strung around his neck.

"Happy Mardi Gras," She said to her barstool friend. "I'm RoRo, and you are…?" She offered her hand in a standard DQ, close to her chest, half-cupped horizontal fashion.

"Glenn." He said in a polite but reserved--I'm not into Queens--tone. But he did grasp her hand and squeeze it ever so slightly. RoRo, difficult as it was, held her tongue.

Cookie Crumbles

"Oh, I'm sorry, Happy Mardi Gras to you too!" Glenn said.

"So, is this your first Fat Tuesday in New Orleans?"

"No, I was born and raised right here in the Quarter but I moved to Texas fifteen years ago. My family is still here." Glenn said.

Out on the balcony, Ginger moved to the end closest to Bourbon Street. The pools of light and shadow cast by the fitful globes of old street lamps made the scene even more romantic than one would expect. Especially after soaking it up for many many Carnival seasons, yet it always seemed to reinvent itself. As she walked to the corner of the balcony and moved down the cross street side of the building the unmistakable pungent scent of quality reefer tugged her nose toward a young man standing alone.

He was muscled, but not gnarly, wearing a tight red tank top, cargo shorts and sandals. His hair was short except for long sweeping bangs hanging to the left. He had two small gold hoops in left ear and one in his right. He took another long deep drag on his joint, held the smoke hard in his chest and let it out with an audible sigh. He saw Ginger staring at him and looked back. Directly.

He spoke.

"My friends are eating Chinese across the way" He said, pointing to the all night restaurant across St. Anne. "You ever eat there?" He asked, offering Ginger the fat, but now much shorter doobie. She took a deep hit and handed it back.

"They tell me I have--couldn't swear to it. That's the way it goes at Mardi Gras you know. Why aren't you with your friends?"

"Not hungry. Not now. Thought I'd get a drink."

"A drink? You seem to have missed both the downstairs and the upstairs bars on your way out to the balcony here." Said Ginger.

"Yeah, I guess…this is a gay bar, isn't it?"

"Yup."

"I'm straight, I mean, just so you know, ah, my girlfriend, my girlfriend is over there, eating chicken fried rice or maybe egg foo yung, I think she likes that too. I'm from Michigan, Grand Rapids. We--I mean the five of us--decided to come down last night, drove straight through...and"

"Of course you are, now shut up and do what you came here to do."

Ginger unzipped her little pants and motioned for the sexy straight boy to extract her dick from her shorts. At his touch it began a very quick inflation like a one-lunged WW2 mae west vest.

"Um, that's big." The boy said.

"Don't let it scare you sweetie, it's harmless, mostly..." Said Ginger...grinning.

✦✦✦✦

Surprisingly RoRo found that the reserved Glenn was actually quite talkative. RoRo had asked a few perfunctory questions and got out of the way.

"I started out in software. I was working for HP, in Dallas. A friend unexpectedly lost his lover, it was a traffic accident, he was walking under the highway north of Dallas on 75, and they have these "slingshots" where you can do a U-turn without even slowing down. So the cars are doing fifty, sixty miles an hour and my friend's lover was just splat--up against an overpass pylon. At least he never felt a thing." Said Glenn in a rush to get all the words out which was so unlike his normal self.

"I'm so sorry." Said RoRo.

"Thanks. It was a long time ago. Clarence, that was my friend's name, was so distraught that he couldn't handle making the arrangements. Since they're from the East Coast they didn't have any family in Texas so I said I'd go with him to the funeral home."

"That was very kind of you."

Glenn was somewhat perplexed by the queen he was chatting with. He had assumed she was a working girl or at least working a hustle of some kind but here they had been talking for quite a while and she had never even mentioned sex once. She seemed genuinely interested in what he had to say.

"While we were in the casket room, dithering over which one to buy, what color, what lining, all those crappy decisions; I was hit with a full blown totally realized concept for a funeral inventory control program." Glenn said.

"What?" Said RoRo eyes very wide.

"Yeah, I know, too creepy for words, right?"

"Kinda/sorta as we say back home. So did you write it?"

"I did. In three months it was up and running. I licensed the product to my first client a month after that. In fact it was the first application specific software for the industry. Five years later I sold my company for enough money to keep me for the rest of my life." Glenn said.

Glenn suddenly realized that he had said a lot more than he should have. He wondered what she would say next?

"Wow, so what were your inputs?" RoRo asked.

Glenn was taken by surprise by her question. He hadn't expected a technical response.

"Well, I really built a statistical model of the area, demographics, income distribution, education level, number of competitors, actuarial data, all the sales data for the previous ten years."

"I'm impressed." She said.

✥✥✥✥✥

Over in the alcove off the top of the stairway MaryAnn and Cal got down to some serious play with the leather boy. They made a perfect tableau of people just getting along without regard for minor considerations like false modesty and hard-edged sexual categories. On the other hand they were drunk and horny.

MaryAnn pulled back her skirt, freed her rod from her lacy panties and

Cookie Crumbles

began to slide it into the hot boy's candy slot. Meanwhile with Calista busy kissing her lipstick off, the harness boy was tuning her nipples up and down a virtual FM band. Cal was trying to get herself situated to take advantage of the sock puppet. Luckily for all three a giant fern hid them from the bartenders sight, but since he was working a twelve stool bar alone--not to mention the balcony--he didn't have a lot of free time to gawk anyway.

Just as things were getting truly interesting between the impromptu threesome a very large leather man holding a braided leash with a big chrome collar hook came up the stairs.

"So there you are Winston. I thought you'd run off. And you found playmates, how nice for you, hmmmm; I'm going to have to punish you now--OK--later. You didn't ask permission, did you?" said the man as he clicked the leash onto Winston's collar.

"No Sir! Sorry Sir!" he said. Master and Winston made their way back downstairs without as much as a bye-bye to MaryAnn and Calista who were left standing rather forlorn, like a kid with a Xmas robot and no batteries. MaryAnn tried to pull her skirt down but it was a futile gesture, at least for a while.

Ginger, with an empty cocktail glass and a big--satisfied--grin, came back into the barroom from the balcony. MaryAnn rushed up to her.

"So, you ready? Let's go." said MaryAnn to Ginger "our friend in the harness, before we got real friendly, mentioned that we could score some X at the Congo Lounge."

"Where'd he go?"

"Oh, he had another engagement." Said MaryAnn.

"I gotta go pee," said Cal.

"Collect RoRo on your way back, OK?" said MaryAnn as the two of them headed for the stairs.

+++++

Cookie Crumbles

Glenn was--surprisingly--having a good time chatting with the garrulous queen. He usually found their innate flamboyance too annoying to bear. He bought her another drink. She told him that her cup of poison was Cuervo 1800, on the rocks, with two limes. The two limes were important, apparently.

"I don't think I've seen any other medallions this season quite like the ones around your neck." Said RoRo.

"That's because I designed them and had them custom made." Said Glenn.

RoRo had taken a liking to Glenn…and it had nothing to do with the revelation that he was rich. She was all in favor of empty meaningless sex, as long as she at least came. But these days, what she really liked--what she was looking for, was the possibility, just that, the possibility--of finding someone to get long-term with, and that prospect became more and more remote as the calendar pages of her life flew--in a 1940's Hollywood style blizzard--off stage and beyond retrieval.

Cal appeared at RoRo's elbow and said, "Hey girlfriend, we're heading out, let's go, let's go, Ginger and MaryAnn are downstairs already."

Without waiting for an answer she split.

RoRo weighed her options. She didn't want to leave the bar stool she occupied. She knew it was crazy but she felt some connection with this guy she'd known for all of thirty minutes. She also felt the tug of Mardi Gras protocol, Cal and Ginger were bound to get completely smashed before the night was squeezed out of the Quarter and MaryAnn was a virgin. She felt an, unwarranted, but palpable obligation to stick together. She decided a different tack.

"Glenn, I'd love it if you came with us on our pub-crawl." She said with emphasis.

Glenn didn't answer immediately, for a moment he leaned into saying that he'd come, but it was already well past 0100 and his innate sense of balance pulled him back.

Cookie Crumbles

"No, no I think I'll have to pass, thanks for the invite though. Have fun."

RoRo felt the sting of that response, wanted to ask again, but didn't.

"Oh, that's OK, no biggie." She toyed with her drink, hoping he'd ask her to stay, but he didn't. She took out her compact and checked her lipstick for the 500th time that night. Shoved it back into her purse and slid off the barstool.

"It was a pleasure making your acquaintance Glenn." She said holding out her hand.

He took it in both his hands and kissed it after giving it a long squeeze. He took one of the beautiful medallions off his neck and put it over RoRo's head. Then he lightly kissed her on the mouth.

"Happy Mardi Gras baby girl." He said.

She sniffed, twice, smiled and made her way downstairs. The gang had already left the bar and was standing outside on the sidewalk waiting for RoRo to pop up.

"Well, where's your guy?" Cal asked.

"He was indisposed to continue our interview for further intimacy." RoRo answered in what she hoped was a lighthearted bit of banter to cover what she knew to be a wildly over the top sense of disappointment.

"Oh! Sorry honey, shit, men are such assholes, his loss!" said Ginger.

"How many blocks up?" Asked RoRo.

"Two or three." Said MaryAnn.

Three blocks later they stood at the edge of the Quarter, on Ramparts.

"Which way do we go?" Ginger asked.

"Ah, I'm not sure. He said two or three blocks up and one or two over."

"I don't see much toward Esplanade, I say we go toward Canal." RoRo proposed.

To the left, down a few doors was a big dingy all night liquor store, but just past that was a dark lobby with neon Day-Glo signs advertising live music for a two drink minimum. The thrum of electric guitars was palpable on the skin.

Cookie Crumbles

"A two drink minimum in here is going to be at least 12 or 13 bucks" said Ginger. "Are you sure this is the place? There's no name."

"We could ask." Said MaryAnn reasonably.

"Ask? That would be so uncool." Said RoRo.

"Well, make up your fuckin' minds girls, cause I gotta pee again." Said Calista.

"I say we cut this joint loose and just go to Ziggy's…I mean we ALWAYS have a good time at Ziggy's. Remember the year that the sweater queen did a floorshow, complete with cartwheels AND splits? That was beyond too cool." Said RoRo. "Besides it's only like three blocks down Ramparts."

"OK with me." Said Ginger.

"Go now!" Cal urged.

MaryAnn was silent but began walking in the direction that RoRo indicated. In very short order the bar they knew as Ziggy's from years past was in full view only now the large sign in the window plainly stated "The Congo Lounge". Everyone started laughing like they'd all been sucking nitrous oxide for an hour.

The Congo Lounge was crowded but not packed. There were two seats at the end of the bar that were open so the four revelers moved to occupy them. RoRo and Cal perched while Ginger and MaryAnn stood behind.

"I'll get the first round." Said Ginger

The bartender was a tall, very shapely and quite pretty M2F trans.

"Hey, happy Mardi Gras y'all, welcome to Congo Lounge. If my back is to ya and you're thirsty just call out Veronica and I'll come running."

"Cool, she's RoRo," said Cal pointing, "that's Ginger, the pretty one there is MaryAnn and I'm Calista."

"Nice to meet all y'all." Said Veronica.

Veronica brought the drinks and Ginger dug some money out of her fanny pack.

"Keep the change honey."

Cookie Crumbles

"Thanks."

Further down the bar Veronica asked a couple of patrons to move over a seat or two and suddenly there was room for the four friends to sit together. Veronica waved them into their new stools. They all expressed their thanks and Veronica smiled in acknowledgement.

RoRo was uncharacteristically unchatty, MaryAnn was trying to scope out exactly who in the bar might be the one the leather boy talked about being way into X, Ginger was still in post bj bliss and Calista seemed to have completely chilled out from her nastiness with Sami.

They all noticed the blonde harem girl about the same time. She was halfway down the bar and was giving people massages--very good massages if the look of relaxation and pleasure her hands left in their wake was any indication.

She was dressed in forest green silky pantaloons that rode very low on her hips, voluptuous hips that resembled, more than anything, a full sized stand up bass, on top she wore a gold satin bolero jacket over a black lacey demi-bra. The pantaloons were split on the outside from just above the ankles to a point where a person, if so inclined, could judge the style of panties that she preferred.

She moved to the unheard sound of castanets clicking off the rhythm of her rolling gait.

As she finished her last massage, she skipped the intervening stools and came up to Ginger and placed her hands on the small of her back, thumbs and fingertips lightly playing over the fabric of her shirt. Ginger paid for a regular massage back home and she was thinking that this girl was the equal of any of the professionals that she used.

"Feel good?" She asked.

"Oh yes, you don't have to stop, please."

Calista was sitting next to Ginger and when she saw the response to the girl's fingers sweep over her friend's face, she wanted to get her turn under those talented hands sooner rather than later.

Cookie Crumbles

"Why did you skip those other people?" Cal asked.

"Oh, I didn't skip them, they already had their Mardi Gras massage before you got here. Only one to a customer."

"I'm sorry, I don't mean to distract you." Said Calista.

"No worries, I'm able to let my hands work on their own while I attend to other business."

Ginger did not speak at all other than some assorted groans and sub vocalizations.

"Does that feel better now honey? You had some really ugly knots in your back."

"I know--back home I have a massage therapist and a chiropractor on retainer. But I feel great now!" Said Ginger.

"OK, now do me, do me!" Said Cal, bouncing on her stool.

"Oh all right--but don't you want the massage first?" Giggled the girl.

"Whoa…well then, we need to introduce ourselves, don't we? I'm Calista…" She said extending her hand.

"Pleased to meet you, my friends call me Sammy." She said, taking the proffered hand and squeezing it gently.

Cal's eyes got big and her face flushed thinking, "How weird is that?" and feeling that rush of anger all over again. But just as quickly it dissipated, she figured, hmmm, second time at bat, OK.

"Seems to be a popular name this Mardi Gras. I tell you I got one hell of a stiff neck, Sammy, been like that for ten years--if you can make me feel better I'll love ya forever!"

Cal could feel Sammy's breasts roll against her back as the girl with magic fingers went to work loosening and tweaking her neck. It was truly a unique experience; this girl was unlike any other masseuse she had ever encountered. As Sammy's fingers found their purchase she leaned in very very close to Calista and her long wavy blonde hair seemed to envelope the girls in a golden cloud.

"That feels good don't it baby? All that stiffness, all that tension is

Cookie Crumbles

gone, like it never happened. When I let you go you're gonna feel like you could do a LindaBlair 360, but I wouldn't advise it!"

Now it was Calista that was moaning and groaning, in some sort of ecstasy. Sammy slowed her ministrations she didn't want to abruptly stop. Cal's eyes had closed at some point.

Cal moved her head from side to side, completely free of stiffness and no pops or clicks as she normally felt and heard. The Lounge had a really good jukebox and it was playing some danceable music.

"Hhhmmmmmm thank you Sammy," Cal purred as she took the blonde's hands in her own, "Come dance with me, OK?"

"Sure, I like to dance. But I've got to tell you, or maybe I already did, that I'm a married woman, flirty but married."

"Sure, right, whatever…" Said Cal unconvinced.

The girls fit together like two pieces of a jigsaw puzzle as they flowed across the floor whispering and giggling. Cal molded herself to Sammy's back, her hands tracing the magnificent curves that filled her pantaloons. Now it was her turn to roll her breasts across the other girl's back.

An attractive young man slipped onto MaryAnn's empty barstool, he was just as blonde and in his own way, as pretty as the harem girl masseuse. RoRo realized that she was the only one left sitting at the bar as her friends and Sammy had all disappeared somewhere. RoRo was considering saying hello or something even more clever to the young man occupying MaryAnn's seat, but he spoke first.

"Have you seen Sammy lately?" He asked.

"I think she's dancing with Calista."

"Oh, figures. Pardon my bad manners, I'm Jimmy."

"RoRo."

"…Pleasure." Said Jimmy.

"So, where are you and your sister from?"

"Sister? Sammy is my wife."

"Really? You look so much alike. And she seems so, ummm, how can I

Cookie Crumbles

put it? Single…"

"Yeah! You're not the first one to point that out. Well, the blonde bombshell who was all over your friend the brunette is really my wife, as much as we look like siblings. She is the world's most outrageous flirt, especially after a few drinks. We're from New Mexico; well that's our mailing address at least. We're really from New Jersey."

"And you were overcome by a irresistible urge to move to New Mexico?" Asked RoRo.

"Irresistible? Yeah, falling off a cliff like Wylie Coyote'--freefall. I was in software, telecom, after being unemployed for two years we decided that Sammy could melt muscle knots anywhere and maybe a change of scenery would do me a world of good."

"And did it?"

"Not really. Instead of working at Home Depot in Parsippany I'm working at Borders in Santa Fe."

"Sorry." Said RoRo. "Let me buy you a drink. Hey Veronica…"

Three shots of tequila later RoRo knew more than she ever wanted to about Jimmy and Sammy including Jimmy's inability to deal with the taste of muff. Eventually Jimmy wandered off--staggered is such a pejorative term--in search of his wife. Drunk as they both seemed to be; RoRo wondered how they were ever going to drive back to their campsite in Hammond; Jimmy had said they hadn't been able to get a hotel in New Orleans so they were roughing it. Roughing it to RoRo meant "no cable", not "no bed".

+++++

RoRo sat alone pouting. She was kicking herself for leaving Glenn back at Good Friends. It seemed so long ago. Throughout the evening she had worked herself up into a very very horny mood. She fingered the medallion he had given her and lost herself in a drunken--one of those 'what might

Cookie Crumbles

have been'--reveries. Jimmy, the erstwhile husband of Samantha, had been an amusing diversion for a short while but it was obvious that talk was the only thing that Jimmy was interested in doing, at least with RoRo. And as Jimmy had got drunker he seemed to be a lot less fun. To be honest, more like a mean drunk--like RoRo's father, who once threw a knife at her in a drunken stupor.

Ginger, MaryAnn and Cal were all deeply into the post 3 AM hustle. Sammy and Cal were lightly making out at the far end of the bar. The girls performed a little impromptu tongue ballet, fully out of the mouth, dainty tip to dainty tip, with a bunch of soulful looks.

Calista suddenly left Samantha and made her way over to the bar where RoRo sat.

"Hey girlfriend, you still have my cigs right? Asked Cal.

"Yup." She said digging thru her purse.

RoRo began to toss the pack to Cal.

"No babe, just the one. Keep the rest. If I have them I'll smoke 'em to nothing before ya know it and then I'll have to go find another pack...K?"

"No problem." Said RoRo.

Cal went back to Samantha.

RoRo was thinking that Calista was never at a loss for companionship; the earlier contretemps at the Corner Pocket notwithstanding--yes, she was jealous--she figured Cal could pick someone up even if they were at the Star Wars cantina. RoRo, on the other hand, never seemed to have easy pickins, unless of course you included trolls, both tranny chasers and the actual trolls that live under bridges. Although Charles--he lived under an overpass on I-94 in Chicago--was more than a perfect gentleman. And he did save RoRo's life, so thankfulness must be demonstrated to show the Gods that you appreciate their intersession. She sighed, another time, another place...

She caught the eye of Veronica and asked for yet another drink even though she should have switched to Diet Coke at least three drinks back.

Cookie Crumbles

Ginger was sitting at a table across the room chatting up the Mad Hatter, after a while RoRo realized that the Hatter was a girl…so Ginger wasn't on the make after all. Try as she might, she couldn't locate MaryAnn in the bar. Probably been successful hunting down that X.

A blast of now cold wet river air entered the bar just ahead of the man filling the doorway. He was enormous, way over six feet tall, olive complexion and quite handsome RoRo decided. He was wearing both a black leather trench coat and a big mullet. RoRo smiled at that anachronism. The coat flapped open revealing a tight white t-shirt tucked into his jeans, hinting at a taut belly and, oddly enough, a pair of handcuffs hanging from his empty belt loops either side of his zipper.

The new arrival scanned the room and as his eyes tracked RoRo they locked on and a huge smile appeared on his face. He pointed to her and said "Mon amour, you are so very cute, may I sit? My name is Atlas…and I must know your name."

"RoRo."

"I couldn't believe it when I saw you sitting here, alone, it is a crime for a beautiful girl like you to be alone, and on Mardi Gras itself! And why are you umm, at home they say 'make a bahbin' how you say, pouting? Please tell me you aren't married and if you are, then please lie…."

He was a master at dishing bullshit, but it was just the tonic that our girl needed. And at that last bit of puffery, RoRo laughed out loud.

"Definitely not married."

The conversation moved rapidly. Atlas was from Houma and he was working the oilrigs in the Gulf, he was Cajun of course and lived for a good party so in Mardi Gras season he headed for 'En Ville', New Orleans to anyone not from the bayous.

Atlas got Veronica's attention and bought a double shot of Jack for himsel

"Laissez les bons temps rouler!" He said as he handed RoRo her drink.

"Let the good times roll!" She answered and downed it.

Cookie Crumbles

"Ah, you know French?"

"Nope but I know party!!"

Calista showed up for another cigarette, after a brief introduction to Atlas and an even briefer reference to oilrigs and the bayous she beat a hasty retreat knowing how depressed her dear friend had felt after getting the brush-off at Good Friends and seeing her almost giddy now.

Atlas asked RoRo to switch stools so he could lean against the wall. As he took the seat she stood between his legs and they were nose to nose. Atlas leaned towards her slightly and she pursed her lips and fell on him hungrily.

All that pent up sexual energy from the long day of titillation came pouring out in a rush and she began to let herself go. She was disconnecting the brain from the sexual id.

The bartender had reduced the number of lights in the room to create a more convivial atmosphere and the corner now occupied by Atlas and RoRo was virtually private. For which they took full advantage.

After kissing off most of her lipstick, RoRo took out her compact to refresh her lip color. She had turned toward the bar to get the most light possible to reflect off her compact's mirror. And when she turned back to Atlas she saw that his rather fully plumped penis was staring up at her.

"Gaienne--that means girlfriend--this is my little buddy, I call him podna. And just look what you've done to him, he's wicked hard. Go ahead; wrap that pretty girly hand around him. Careful of those nails now."

RoRo had never actually seen an uncut cock before, knowing Atlas' culture to be heavily Catholic she asked, "How come you were never circumcised?"

"Mais mon amour, my pawpaw was not a big fan of the black cassocks.. He stopped going to church long before I was born, my mama always went but he wouldn't let her take me."

"Were you even baptized?"

Cookie Crumbles

"Mais oui, granmama did that herself, I was born on our kitchen table."

RoRo couldn't put it off any longer. She had broken a rule; you know the one, one tequila, two tequila, three tequila, floor? Well the floor was still under her heels and not her nose but put it this way, she was way over the limit and she was cruising on autopilot.

She had to pee and that was a hassle that she dreaded. Since she was currently in serious lip lock with Atlas, not to mention giving his uncut totally lovely member a hand job, careful, as Atlas had made clear, of the blood red talons she wore; she needed to diplomatically extricate herself and make her way to the little girl's room.

"I need to relieve myself, darling. I'll be a while, what with all the layers, hooks, snaps and shit. I'll be right back though…"

There was no way he could tuck himself back into his pants. As he was sitting with his back to the wall, RoRo, standing between his legs, had effectively blocked the view of anyone watching. She took a Mardi Gras colored plastic top hat that someone had left on the bar and popped it over Atlas' hardon. She grabbed her purse and headed for the restroom.

"Guess you'll have to hang on to your hat." She said laughing.

He groaned.

Atlas grew more and more frustrated waiting for RoRo to return. He had another double shot of Jack while he tried to chill. His penis refused to subside. Taking the Viagra earlier in the evening might have been a bad decision, pissing off Darlene and getting thrown out of their hotel room was even worse.

Wearing his top hat on his little head he walked the length of the bar towards the restrooms.

Well, make the best of it, he thought, always had wondered what it would be like doing a tranny…

RoRo stood at the vanity and powdered her shiny nose, which made her think of Rudolph the Reindeer and in her stupor she giggled like she was watching Saturday Night Live in the days of the Bassomatic. The door

Cookie Crumbles

opened to reveal a decidedly pissy looking Atlas standing there with that stupid top hat still grappled to his groin.

"You been gone a half-hour mon amour." He said.

"Oh sugar, it's only been a few minutes, I told you I'd be right back, and as you can see I'm almost done."

"You be done…"

RoRo bent over to pick up her purse but Atlas grabbed her arm and dragged her out the Women's and into the Men's room.

"You got me stiff as a priest at a cub scout meeting--you gon' fix it, NOW."

"OK, Mr. Man, I told you I'd take care of it. When I waitressed at a truck stop back home, one of my best customers was a good ol' boy from Dallas--he always said I could suck the chrome off a trailer hitch."

With that she tossed the top hat in the corner wrapped her fingers thru the loops of Atlas' jeans like a bronco rider grabbing the horse's mane and buried her not shiny nose in his crotch.

"I don't think so, mon fille. I'm all for a hummer when it's right, but I'm not interested now. I'm fixing to bury my little podna right in your hot back door pussy."

Atlas used the handcuffs to capture RoRo's wrists, opened the stall door and hung the poor girl like a side of beef ready to be steaks.

"Listen you big lug, I don't want you fucking me--do you hear me? My ass is not for you, I said NO…"

Atlas reached under RoRo's skirt, pulled her Frederick's padded panties off and stuffed them into her mouth. RoRo was reduced to a mostly inaudible growl.

"Where the hell did that damn girl go with my cigarettes?" asked Calista to no one in

particular.

Cal entered the Women's restroom, saw it was empty, but noted RoRo's purse on the floor and shouted "RoRo, where the fuck did you go?"

Cookie Crumbles

No answer, but a dull thumping came from the Men's next door. Cal was no stranger to the Men's room in more than one establishment, so she put her shoulder to the door and banged it open. The scene she witnessed was very disturbing.

The toilet stall door stood full open and RoRo was handcuffed and hanging from the coat hook. It was far enough off the floor that RoRo was on tippy toes and unable to lift her arms any higher to free herself. The thumping Cal heard was the result of RoRo slamming the door against the wall repeatedly.

"Hey! Swamp boy! I don't think she wants to play with you! Let her down."

"Stay out of this! She got me all horny, had her hands all over me and my podna and I'm done playing. 'Sides--she wants it as bad as I do!"

"Oh? Is that why her panties are stuffed in her mouth?" asked Cal.

"Get the fuck out of here, this is none of your concern. Go to the Women's and do your pouponer, powder your face!"

"Listen, I think you're too fucking drunk to grasp what you're doing! She doesn't want you to fuck her in the ass, she DOESN'T WANT IT--capiche?"

Atlas ignored her. Cal weighed her options. The guy easily had over a hundred pounds on her not to mention a foot or so of reach. She had heard him say at one point--when she got a cigarette--that he was an oil platform roustabout and he had the muscle mass to prove it. Here he was--about to drill her dearest friend. He didn't look too gentle and by the time she left and got back with help, RoRo could be much the worse for wear.

RoRo was not cooperating and the husky Cajun was having trouble penetrating a moving target. In the struggle to control the big ol' girl that RoRo is, Atlas' pants had completely come undone and puddled around the ankles of his jet-black fancy tooled cowboy boots. He had gone out commando style and Cal saw his big white nut sack slapping against her pal's ass and suddenly had an inspiration.

Cookie Crumbles

Cal grabbed Atlas' testicles in her right hand and squeezed for all the strength she had. RoRo's assailant screamed and collapsed into a twitching heap on the wet tile floor. She pushed the stall door closed so that RoRo could get her feet on the toilet and free herself from the coat hook. Cal began to search for the handcuff key with her free hand.

"Oh, what do we have here?" Cal said examining the inside of Atlas' left boot. "A 45 caliber two shot derringer just like my daddy used to have, hmmmn."

The watch pocket had the key to the cuffs and RoRo was soon unencumbered.

Whether or not Atlas had actually passed out from the pain was an open question, but Calista kept a secure hold on his balls, ready to fire off another punishing jolt if needed.

"Listen up! I can frog-march you half naked through the bar to the street after I squeeze the shit outa you one more time, or you can pull up your pants and get the hell out of here and never let us see you again. Your choice." Said Cal. "Oh, and don't forget I found your derringer."

Atlas slowly got to his feet, pulled up his pants and left, limping, without a sound or a backward glance. RoRo swore she was all right, got her panties back on, dropped the handcuffs into her purse and continued thanking Cal for saving her.

"Cal?"

"Yeah honey?"

"Can we just keep this little incident between us? I feel so stupid. I got way too drunk.

I mean I don't even think he was that bad a guy, well he sure wasn't a good guy...Oh shit, I'm a mess. But the adrenaline buzz got me clean sober now. I'm kinda embarrassed, ya know?"

"I won't tell a soul. I have my price though."

"Yeah?"

"Yup, you gotta lay off mothering me like you always do, I'm a big girl, and I think I proved it tonight!"

"No argument there, deal!" She said, extending her arms for a big hug. Which she received.

As Cal walked to the bar where she had left Samantha--Ginger and MaryAnn came up to announce that they were starving and had to eat now.

"Ginger, I'm all for that. It's time to leave, really past time, can you go out and flag us a cab?" Said Cal thinking that just maybe Atlas might be lurking about outside looking to continue the previous conversation and if he were, he wouldn't connect Ginger with RoRo or herself.

"Sure girl, come on MaryAnn, we're leaving. Listen Cal, that Samantha girl is wanting to talk to you." Said Ginger.

"Oh, OK…"

Cal and RoRo walked up to the Jukebox where Samantha and Jimmy were having a very heated argument.

"…And I told you--at least ten times--I'm not ready to go back to Hammond yet." Said Sam.

"Well I am, I'm bored shitless--I haven't been making out with half the freaks in this bar like you have."

"That's a little harsh, don't you think Jimmy?" said Cal.

Samantha whirled around, "Oh there you are, I was bumming, thought you'd left without saying good-bye."

"I wouldn't have done that! I may be a freak, like your terribly rude husband says, but I do have my manners."

MaryAnn appeared, "Hey, cabs waiting!"

"Samantha, I'm not asking again, you coming?" said Jimmy making a move for the door.

"We're gonna catch some dinner at the St Charles Tavern, why don'cha come with?" said Cal. "Well, more like breakfast at five in the morning I guess."

"Well, where…" Said Sam.

Cookie Crumbles

"I'm out of here." Said Jimmy over his shoulder.

No one said 'stop, don't go'...

"...Where would I sleep?" Asked Sam.

"Ummm, with me?" Said Cal, dimpled and twinkling like the night sky in the middle of nowhere.

"But--but, I'm not a lesbian..."

"Oh that's all right honey, neither am I!" said Calista breezily as she drew Sammy to her and kissed her soundly on her rather generous mouth.

"I said, the cab's waiting!" Shouted MaryAnn at the door. "I'm hungry, dammit..."

Cookie Crumbles

Wet and Wild

In an age when children were not raised with the expectation that serial killers stalked every neighborhood life was a much less regulated exercise. I want to give you a flavor of what mine was like--when there were only three television networks and their signals went dark every night at midnight.

When my father was a young man he was kidnapped and held for ransom for six years by the US Government. During this period he was a machine gunner in Pacific island real estate disputes, he also passed a few months with the headhunters in New Guinea. He visited other garden spots with his captors, ending in the Australian Outback. Eventually, in the manner of 'The Ransom of Red Chief', they grew tired of him and he was released. While he wanted to stay in the Outback and groom sheep a family crisis forced him back to his hometown of Milwaukee.

It was there that he met my mother. She was the middle daughter of an Italian hardhat diver. He met her at some kind of social function with a live band. He asked her if she wanted to dance. She answered "No, I came all the way across town on two different street cars just to chat with my girlfriend here who lives across the alley from my house." Their relationship continued in this vein for 35 years.

Every event chronicled here is true at some level of abstraction. I was born into an upper middle class family. There was a thriving construction business, there was money in the bank, there were two brand new cars in the garage, and there was Eisenhower on television. By the time I was 13 we were dead broke. I knew things were tough because I started getting lettuce sandwiches in my Howdy-Doody lunchbox. This was way before white people started eating tacos. But I'm getting ahead of the story.

My very first memory is staring at my grandmother's chandelier. I was

Cookie Crumbles

staring straight at it; eye to bauble and it was hanging a foot from the ceiling. As is common with grandfathers, mine delighted in throwing me up in the air as high as he could and then catching me, repeatedly. This made me scream, it made my mother and grandmother scream too. It made my grandfather laugh. My grandfather never gave a fuck what other people thought. Unfortunately this attitude extended to his doctor. He died at 54, the victim of a broken heart, not emotionally, mechanically. One day it just stopped. He was my mother's father. He died when I was 3 or 4 so all I really remember about him are the flight lessons, the rest are imported memories. My father's father lived decades longer and I learned many important lessons from him.

Thinking of that chandelier I guess you could say I started out on a high note and tried to stay that way ever after. I'm the crazy type, I love life and nothing is more fun than being scared to death. Do you know what an adventure is? It's when you risk your life for no apparent reason and live to laugh about it later. It's the feeling that you get when you have one chance to get it right, with no makeup test.

If my mother's father was a pillar of light, the life of the party, my father's mother was his polar opposite, a pillar of salt. She was consumed with appearances, following the rules and making her sister eat dirt. I could imagine her handling the reins of a Conestoga wagon lumbering across the high plains. She was a French-Canadian woman from far northern Wisconsin, strong and husky. She knew her own mind, at least until she lost it. Opinions vary as to when that happened. I'll tell you about the day she taught me to swim.

We lived on a lake in a rather grand house compared to rest of the neighborhood. My family had bought a little frame cottage and morphed it into a six-bedroom manor with a two and half car garage and a concrete driveway and a gate. We had frontage property on the lake itself with a pier and a boat ramp. In the back yard, which closely resembled a rain forest our property ended at the bank of a canal. I was four years old and my unescorted romps in the woods and swamps entailed a certain measure of risk. Grandmother was insistent that I learn to swim. My mother said that my dad would take me down to the lake and teach me to swim as soon as he had time. More than a few days passed with no instructions and my grandmother lost her patience. My dad had almost died as a very young child and that event fiercely colored her attitude toward my safety.

Saturday morning [I knew it was Saturday because it was cartoon day on the TV] she strode into the living room and told me to go get my swimming trunks.

"I'm going to teach you to swim," she said.

I raced upstairs and changed as quick as I could, I didn't want to keep her waiting. She was well on her way to the pier and I ran to catch up. My mother and father were still on the porch and I heard my Dad ask my Mom what was going on? The water at the end of the pier was about four feet deep and I was about three feet tall. She was standing at the edge where the half tires provided cushion to the docking boats. I skidded to a halt, oblivious to splinters. She scooped me up while I was still wobbling and tossed me high in the air over the water.

As I arced into the lake I managed to rotate so that I hit the greenish water face first and since I was hollering in wide-eyed terror my open mouth dredged a half-gallon of water. I righted myself below the surface and attempted to stand but my feet sank into the cold viscous muck. It sucked the heat out of my body to my knees. I instinctively kicked away from the bottom and felt my fingertips break the surface of the water; I redoubled my efforts and broke the surface cleanly, arms flailing, and lungs furious. As I sucked sweet oxygen my thrashing arms took on a more regular rhythm and I re-invented the dogpaddle.

"What do you think you are doing?" my grandmother asked.

"I don't know." I said.

Cookie Crumbles

"Swimming." She replied. "Now swim over to the next pier and back."

She stood waiting on the pier until I bobbed back at my starting point.

"Fine, you'll never forget this--or how to swim" she said as she turned and walked back to the house. My parents, still perplexed, stepped onto the pier as she left it.

"What's going on?" My mother asked.

"He swims now."

As my mother ran down the pier I climbed back up and flung myself into the water, careful this time to not let my feet touch the muck. After I regained the wooden dock a second time, my mother marched me off the pier and back to the house. I watched as my father and grandmother yelled at each other about parenting responsibilities. Long before I read Darwin I knew the essence of life was struggle.

❖❖❖

By the time I was six my best friend in the whole world was Shaw. He lived in the swamp a quarter mile down the road from our house. We were always together. All the locals thought he was weird; but I thought he was brilliant. I was his only friend.

Shaw lived with his family in a ramshackle house that looked to be sinking into the swamp. There was a flat-bottomed skiff up on the porch leaning against the side of the building for when the spring floods cut the house off from the road. Shaw's father actually lived in the garage behind the house. He'd moved out after a hellacious [a neighbor lady recounted the story to my mother one day over coffee] argument that involved kitchen knives. This happened a few years before we moved into the area. As Shaw had younger siblings it seemed that his father visited the house from time to time since there was no gossip about his mom seeing other men.

Even though Shaw was my age he was far more advanced than I. His father made his living as a back yard mechanic and all around handyman. Shaw had inherited his aptitude. Shaw and I would create elaborate dioramas in his backyard. He had the world's largest collection of die cast army men. We would create tableaus with quite varied topology including forests, hills and running streams [fed from an old rusted 55 gallon drum we'd salvaged], then we'd populate it with our soldiers and models of tanks, trucks and artillery. Unfortunately I only had plastic army men. We would spend hours playing war and arguing over battlefield casualties. My army base even had a stage setup for a USO show, I imagined Bob Hope and a half-dozen blonde showgirls. Believe me, the fact that we were actually playing with little green dolls was not lost on me.

I'd gotten the USO idea from my uncle Steve; he'd been in the Marines in the Korean War and I'd heard him talk about such things. The whole family had gotten together for a big party when he came home. He was wearing his uniform with all his medals. I was very impressed.

The very last war game Shaw and I had was on the 4th of July, the summer after we finished first grade. The local Fish and Game Association would always throw big parties at the Firehouse on holidays. Everyone in the village would come and eat burgers and brats and roast corn and drink enormous quantities of beer all afternoon. In between eating and drinking there was gambling.

You could play showdown poker, the Wheel of Fortune or Chuck-a-Luck. The latter was a dice game played mostly by ladies but they let kids play too. You got five dice in a cup and you had five chances to throw five of a kind, it wasn't that hard cause they'd let you build up to it and you could change your mind about what you were shooting for if you wanted to. Anyway, if you won you got a little prize that probably cost a penny. But that summer Shaw and I were excited to the point of frenzy, one of the Chuck-a-Luck prizes was a flat of Black Cat firecrackers, fifty of them,

Cookie Crumbles

all the way from China!

It cost a dime to play and between us we had three bucks, well, I had three bucks cause I got my allowance on Saturday – three bucks a week. Shaw never had any money. I was supposed to put two bucks into my college fund but since it was a holiday I got to spend it all. I was never lucky so I gave Shaw a dime and he played. On his first shake he got two sixes so that's what he went for, but you put the two sixes aside and shoot the remaining three dice…second shake, no sixes, third, nope, fourth shake, one six. The last shake and two dice left, he had to shoot two sixes. He rolled the dice around in the hard leather cup for what seemed like an hour and then finally slammed it down on the green felt. He lifted the cup and snake eyes stared up at us! Damn, a loser, two ones. I guess it wasn't as easy as I thought.

We kept slicing away at my three dollars in 10-cent slivers until I only had half a buck left. Finally lady fortune smiled on us and we nailed 5 deuces and we did it in four shakes, no bonus though, too bad. That's when things went south in a big way. We tried to claim the flat of 50 Black Cat firecrackers but the Chuck-a-Luck manager stopped us in mid-chortle. She told the lady running our little green felt universe that winners had to be 10 years old to take firecrackers for a prize and since she knew full well that we were only in first grade we didn't make the cut. So she gave Shaw an actual metal cap gun with genuine plastic ivory-colored grips and five boxes of ribbon caps. Under normal circumstances it would have been a red-letter day. Instead--we left the firehouse kicking dirt clods into the air, wearing massive amounts of tread off my PF Flyers; Shaw was, of course, barefoot.

Before we'd traveled very far in this state of high dudgeon the fire siren began wailing it's scary ululating bleat. But there was no fire--this time it was announcing the annual fire hose tug of war. At the ball diamond in the rear of the fire house along the first base line, but set well outside the

Cookie Crumbles

runner's path, two telephone poles were planted. Strung between these poles was a heavy four-strand cable and hanging from the cable by two little wheels in a vertical arrangement so it couldn't fly off, was a 25-gallon drum.

A huge crowd was gathering in anticipation of the tug of war. It would feature the volunteer firemen from our own community, Cold Harbor and those stalwart firemen from Lake Seven, just down the road a country mile or two. The official wager on the contest was one full keg of beer but it would not be a surprise to anyone if serious amounts of money were also in play.

As we watched we heard the big old pumper truck roaring across the outfield. The truck was driven by our fire chief, Joyce. As the crowd parted creating a path, the Chief rolled along until she came to a halt at home plate. With a great grinding of gears she put the pumper in reverse and backed up enough to make the truck sit parallel to the cable setup. Joyce got out of the cab of the pumper and climbed up on top of the water tank to address the crowd.

Joyce was 29 years old and she'd had eight kids since she'd gotten married at 15. She was a very capable young woman. When the AMC plant called back everyone they'd layed off for the past three years all the guys who could drive the trucks were on the line working all day. Joyce volunteered to learn to drive the big ladder rig; it was half again as big as the pumper. She learned quickly and the men were impressed, her husband wasn't surprised.

Joyce introduced the two teams of four guys each. Then they attached two three-inch hoses to the water outlets on the tanker and took their positions under the barrel at the center of the cable.

"OK, the only rule is that you can't use the hose on your opponents, ya gotta aim at the barrel, got it?" said Joyce.

"We got it Chief, let's do it!" said one of the guys from Cold Harbor.

Joyce gestured to her oldest son to hit the switch that started charging the pump.

"All right, on the count of three, start hosing! One…two…THREE!!"

For a brief time the barrel just rocked back and forth. Neither team able to really get a purchase on the slick painted cylinder. The air was full of water falling back to the ground and shortly everyone in the tug o war was soaked as the ground turned muddy as the banks of the Little River. Jason, the lead hoser from Lake Seven was gamely trying to keep his feet under him as his teammates began to lose their grip on the bucking fire hose as they ran back and forth in the deepening mud.

That mud sucked one of Jason's sneakers clean off and he went down flat on his face in the sludge after losing his balance. As he went down the hose blasted the lead man of the Cold Harbor team and knocked him off his feet, within seconds all eight men were on the ground with the hoses whipping around like mad boa constrictors. The crowd was convulsed in laughter.

It suddenly occurred to Shaw and me that no one was in the Firehouse. Everyone was totally focused on the utter insanity at the tug o war. Without a word passing between us we turned and ran back into the building we had just left, Shaw scooped up the flat of 50 Black Cats that we had been denied while I quickly checked the stacks of prize boxes looking for more fireworks. I didn't find any and didn't feel comfortable using any more time to search as some adult could return momentarily. Shaw put the package under his shirt and we made our escape.

The tug o war was still suspended as the contestants regained their feet --Joyce had had the presence of mind to cut off the power from the pumper and the hoses had lost their animation. We didn't tarry but instead made a beeline for our own battlefield down the old Lake road to Shaw's house. When we arrived everything was just as we left it, except the reservoir was drained. Shaw went to refill it while I went in search of matches.

It was an intense but short war. My side took the massive brunt of the

Cookie Crumbles

injuries. My brave lads were almost all missing arms or legs. A few free-rolling heads were scattered about. The devastation wrought by the Black Cats we each tossed into the diorama in lieu of artillery shells was horrible--at least in my mind. I suspect that Shaw was quite aware that his metal men would be merely blown out of their foxholes while my troops would be shredded. There was even an acrid scent of gunpowder and burnt cordage hanging over the scene. It began to slowly enter my thoughts that my huge green bag of "100 Man Army" was reduced to an under strength platoon and I'd be hard pressed to explain to my Mom what bad luck had befallen them.

⁕⁕⁕

By the time I completed my house arrest over the firecracker episode, summer vacation was rapidly dwindling to a few golden days. What had seemed to be an eternity of lazy days and unscheduled hours on Memorial Day--sitting in the cool wet grass at the lakefront Veterans Park watching all the neighborhood dads overstuffed into their old Army uniforms shouldering their rifles, firing a triple salute into the rising sun – was now too short to waste a single minute. Soon it would be Labor Day and back to school. Since I already knew how to read, write and do math I was mystified about what exactly second grade had in store for me?

However my main goal for this summer was still unfulfilled and I knew that our July 4th escapade did not make a good case for favors being granted. My mind was a lawyerly one, for a long while I thought a career in the law was attractive. The milieu in which I was raised was very traditional in terms of familial respect. One didn't defy a direct order once given, however being Catholic I was well versed in loopholes and the concept that if an activity was not expressly forbidden then a strong argument could be made that it was allowed.

Shaw was an archetype, the country boy. He harvested night crawlers by

Cookie Crumbles

the light of the moon, he caught bass with a simple cane pole and a single wormy hook, and he stuffed dead animals. He brought Huck Finn to life. I hadn't read Twain yet, but I'd seen the movie. What set Shaw apart was the fact that he never wore shoes unless there was snow on the ground or he was in school. I had raised this issue of going barefoot outside with my mother a number of times. It had been dismissed without even a cursory review.

What could I do? One, I could feel out my grandmother Gen, my father's mother; if she supported the idea I could use it as leverage. Two, I could use the "ask Mom while she is half asleep and I'm on the way out the door" method, generally effective but not to be used lightly. Three, I could enlist my grandfather; if he thought it was a good idea he could simply issue an edict, but that was not to be used unless it was life and death. In the end I decided to simply grind it out – asking almost everyday until maybe, just maybe she'd be in a really good mood and relent.

It turned out that both my grandmother Gen and Mom were adamantly against my going barefoot. In Gen's words:

"Young gentlemen always wear shoes, always."

She had no idea how wrong she was. So I decided that I would be the absolutely perfect child the entire coming week [we had just returned from Sunday mass], I had overheard my Grandmother discussing the fact that she would be attending a retreat at the local monastery next weekend. Once my mother was alone I would have immeasurably better odds of talking her into letting me go barefoot; after all, it was perfectly harmless, what could go wrong?

I did have some fear about the atmosphere in the house after grandmother came home from her retreat. She obsessed about God and the saints; our house was routinely infested with priests and nuns. Grandpa's sister was a nun – Sister Kathleen, the funny thing was he never even went to church, except once a year on Christmas Eve. He never put religion down, he just said he and God had a special relationship and he

Cookie Crumbles

didn't need a building to express it. He did have a rather uncharitable name for the parish priest though; he called him "the octopus" because he said the priest had a hand for every pocket you had.

Whenever grandmother went away to spend time with God it became real tense in the house. She would always return very spiritually militant and it took quite a while to wear off. So my mind was made up, it was this weekend for sure.

My behavior for the time leading up to Saturday was so exemplary that I caught my mother smiling at me more than a few times when she thought I was otherwise engaged. Obviously she thought that the earnest lessons in deportment she provided me had finally bore fruit.

Friday night my grandfather carried his wife's suitcase to a station wagon being driven by Brother Stevens, one of the monks in residence at the great Cathedral built by German stonemasons in 1870 only a few miles from our lake house. It may have been geographically Wisconsin but in spirit it was deep in the Black Forest. My grandmother had been looking forward to this retreat for weeks. We waved goodbye. The wagon slowly rolled in reverse toward the gate. She would come back to us on Monday.

Saturday morning was glorious, a clear blue sky and a hot August sun promised serious heat by midmorning. I was sitting at the kitchen table eating my breakfast cereal while considering my options; I could wake my mother up or wait until she stirred on her own. Mother and I were alone in the house, as the men had left military early for the weekly shopping run to the nearest town, twelve long miles away.

Suddenly a cheerful "Good morning sweetheart!" rang out. My mother floated down the staircase into the kitchen. Knowing her mother-in-law was not in the house considerably lightened her step.

"Hi Mom."

"Do you want me to make you breakfast?" She asked.

"That's OK, I already ate."

"Oh you did, well I'm going to make some French Toast, how about if I

Cookie Crumbles

make an extra piece just in case you develop a sudden urge?"

"I'd like that. Can I mix the egg batter?"

"Thank you, that would be very nice, you've just been so helpful around here lately."

I quickly cracked four eggs into a heavy ceramic bowl, poured a bit of milk in and then a dollop of vanilla extract. I used a whisk to beat the mix into a froth. My Mother was always surprised that I only had to watch her do something in the kitchen once and I could remember it perfectly.

By the time she was done eating her first piece of toast I claimed the 'extra' piece. It was delicious. As I finished the last bite she fixed me with her 'you're not fooling me for a second' stare.

"So my darling, what is it you want? You've been the absolute poster child for every mother's dream this entire week, so – spill it."

"OK. I just want to be like all the other kids!"

"You mean you want to be like Shaw! I shouldn't let you play with him at all. Stealing those firecrackers had to be his idea!"

"We didn't steal them, we won them fair and square!!!"

Suddenly she started to laugh, an uproarious belly laugh that shook her whole body, she laughed so hard she didn't have any breath left to talk.

"That is too precious by half. So much like your grandfather, my father I mean, he was, oh God. Sometimes you remind me so much, he never made excuses, he wouldn't go around a problem, he just went through it, like a bulldozer. All right. I guess this would be the perfect time with grandma Gen being gone."

"You mean it? I can go barefoot?"

"Yes, but you better be careful, you hear me? I…"

She was still talking when the banging of the screen door muffled her words. I kicked off my shoes and stripped my socks as I ran into the back yard. The still dewy blades of grass tickled my feet as I literally jumped for joy. It was so different from shoes weighing you down. I felt I could fly. My only regret was that Shaw was off at some fly-fishing convention in

Cookie Crumbles

the city with his dad. He probably wouldn't even believe me when he got back.

I spent the morning exploring the many hillocks and holes in the swamp. The ground was thick with short spiky grass, separated by patches of lichens that squished when you walked on them. The sinkholes were very wet and some were still full of water even though it hadn't rained for a week. There were areas with sawgrass that was taller than me and I built a little hut by thatching various blades together. The nuns at school had taught us this technique in order to braid leftovers from Palm Sunday into crucifixes that they sold at Holy Name Society smokers.

I stayed away from the canal itself though. The last time I got too close to where the sod stopped and the bank began, I got a couple of leeches on my legs. I ran home screaming for my mother to get them off. I wasn't going to repeat that experience.

After a while I got bored. I remembered an exciting idea I had gotten in church looking at the vaulted ceiling.

The house next door to our property was small but it did have an actual boathouse. I thought that was really neat. I had to clamber over a pretty high wooden fence. The owner had started fixing the boathouse roof weeks before but never finished. There were two trees that were twenty or thirty feet apart on the ground but their upper branches interlaced forming an archway. Last Sunday I wondered if I could traverse the branches to go from tree to tree like Tarzan. I bet not even Shaw had done that!

I decided to climb up the tree on the right and climb down the tree on the left, the one closest to the boathouse. Mostly because the tree on the right was easier to climb. I was up in no time. These trees were really old, the trunk split into three huge branches. I had to climb higher that I'd ever gone before.

As I got to the halfway point my mother came out on the back stoop and called me in for lunch. I had to hurry; I sure didn't want her to see me fifty feet above the ground. As I came down the other tree I saw a pile of

Cookie Crumbles

lumber up against it's exposed roots. I'd have to try to clear it when I came down. I decided to jump from the main split. It wasn't any higher than jumping off Shaw's garage which we'd done plenty of times.

But the tree had a good deal of Spanish moss and as I leaped I lost my footing. I landed on the pile of wood. I knew something was really wrong immediately. My right foot just felt icky.

The intense pain did not really start until I looked down and saw the point of the eight-penny nail sticking out of the top of my foot two inches below where the toes start. I tried to shake the board off but the nail had bent just enough that the wood was stuck fast. My mother was still calling me in for lunch. I had to spin the board until it was parallel with my foot so that I could walk at all. It felt weird to feel the nail turn.

The fence stopped me in my tracks. I couldn't climb over it and I couldn't squeeze under it. My mother finally saw me standing there.

"What are you waiting for?" She asked.

For some reason that simple question triggered a flood of tears and wailing that had been surprisingly absent up to now. While she could not see what was wrong she felt an awful twist in her chest, she ran to me and came over the fence effortlessly. She scooped me up in her arms and started for the street since she couldn't maneuver the fence under a load. The damn board was still attached to me.

As she turned right at the fence line my grandfather's huge 1955 Pontiac screeched to a halt. Dad jumped out and took in the scene with one all-encompassing look. He took me from my mother.

"Get some peroxide and Mercurochrome – bring it to the garage."

He put me on his workbench and used pliers to straighten the nail, and then he gently pulled my foot off the lumber. Mom cleaned the wound and painted it with the Mercurochrome.

"He's going to need a tetanus shot." Grandpa said.

While my mom comforted me on the workbench they quickly unloaded the groceries from the car, very soon we were on the way to the hospital.

Cookie Crumbles

"Well," my grandfather was speaking to my father, "you know this little incident is just the thing your mother will harp on for the next 20 years."

"I know! She is never happy with the way we raise the boy. One day we're too lenient, the next it's--you're going to break his spirit. She's driving Mela crazy."

I could feel my mother tense up. I felt terrible; not from the pain but from knowing that I was responsible for putting my mother in a bad spot. She'd never hear the end of it.

"There is only one good solution to this problem" Grandpa said.

"What?" Both my parents asked the question at the same time.

"There is no reason why your mother needs to know about this, ever. When we get to the highway we'd normally go west to Union Hospital, instead we could go east to Falls Hospital, nobody knows us there. It'll be like it never happened. When grandma Gen gets home, you better not still be limping, understand boy?"

I could feel my mother relax; she was truly dreading a relentless interrogation from her mother-in-law. My father would be of no help.

"Yes sir!!" And the four of us never spoke of it again.

Cookie Crumbles

No Shoulder to Speak Of

Betsy and I preferred our bikes to cars whenever possible. There was no place more plugged in to the zeitgeist back in the 70s than Madison. Every social movement was represented. We were green before it became fashionable, the campus of the University of Wisconsin is so widely scattered that bicycles are a necessity. I met Betsy while we both lived in an old Victorian house on the lakeside end of Butler Street about a mile from the Rathskellar, the main bar in the Student Union. Our relationship was one of those where the 'click' on meeting was audible; we knew immediately that we would be best friends forever. Sadly, forever proved to be short a few zeros.

Our friendship was a symbiotic, mutually beneficial exchange of everything except bodily fluids. We had both come from socially conservative family backgrounds; before we buddied up we were very tentative in exploring what the University experience had to offer. All that changed when we became each other's catalyst. We kept pushing the other to try something new, to take a risk, whether it was as mundane as eating with your fingers in an Ethiopian restaurant or--for the first time--walking into a flashy trashy gay bar. And after each of our little adventures we would fly away home to our big old house and giggle ourselves to sleep.

Butler House was immense, three floors and an attic, the student population must have exceeded the fire code by at least a factor of two. People floated throughout the building pretty much at will and there was always a party going on. One night Betsy and I were sitting on the love seat in the front parlor. The big bay window framed the postcard-like image of Lake Mendota with the moon hanging low in the sky reflecting a pale glow like a gossamer road on the placid waters.

Two guys came in, one lived in the house and he introduced his friend to everyone in the room. The new guy was--unusual. He was dark haired, long enough that it curled at his collar and blue-eyed, movie star good-looking. His jeans fit snugly and suggested taut muscles, especially the rear. With his half-buttoned denim shirt tucked in, he looked tailored. He wore a red bandana tied around his neck and somehow he carried it off. His animal essence was palpable; Betsy and I exchanged a glance that bespoke a mutual desire but not one to be shared.

"Hi, I'm Sam," I said.

"And I'm Betsy."

His name was Barry and he asked if he could sit down. We cleared a middle space and he kicked his backpack under the couch. He told us he'd been traveling around Europe until his money had run out, spending most of the last year in Paris unofficially attending the Sorbonne where Gallic immersion seemed to have slightly inflected his English, affectation or not it charmed the pants off both of us.

Despite his sophistication and excellent grooming it became obvious that he wasn't into guys. I knew he and Betsy would end up together when he stayed awake while she explained how Woodward and Bernstein inspired her career choice. I know, I know, meeow…

Three years later I was the maid of honor at their wedding. My change of gender wasn't quite as uneventful as all that, really, but Betsy stood by me through the whole process and I never regretted the path I walked for a minute.

And I have to say that Barry wasn't just a set of chiseled abs and a good haircut either. He had integrity. After the dessert course had been cleared away at the wedding rehearsal dinner I had been in the ladies room touching up my lipstick.

I stood in the mirror appraising my red silk sheath dress and matching pumps. I was showing just enough cleavage, not crossing into tacky. One of the ushers had given me a very unhurried look and I was considering my response. As I came out into the hallway I saw Barry's mother heading my way. There was something about her gait that told me she was on a serious mission.

Cookie Crumbles

"Samantha," she called to me in a very business like tone of voice. "I'd like a moment to speak with you if I might…"

"Certainly Mrs. Burke."

"Forgive me, but I find this most difficult, distasteful really, but I have to speak my mind. I will not have my son's wedding turned into some kind of freak show by--well, there is no delicate way to say it, by the presence of a drag queen!"

"Well, technically I'm a post op transsexual. Never actually been a drag queen. Never even performed in a gay fundraiser."

"This is no time for frivolous repartee young man!"

"Excuse me Mrs. Burke, I am not now nor have I ever been a man, young or otherwise. I have had a surgical intervention to correct a serious congenital defect. And if you are going to continue the offensive tone of your remarks this conversation is over."

"You are not going to subject my family to ridicule."

"Hhhmmm and just how did you come into possession of this information?"

"I had a background check done on Betsy, you can never be too careful. You figured prominently in the appendix."

"Mrs. Burke, I…"

"Mother!" Barry's voice cut through our exchange like a too quick lick on a stiff envelope flap that cuts your tongue.

"I'm only looking after your interests since you seem unwilling to do it yourself!" She snapped.

"Listen to me! Samantha is Betsy's choice to be her maid of honor. She is a woman who has always conducted herself as a lady and until you read that report you had not the slightest whiff of complaint about her. Give me the file."

Mrs. Burke opened her purse and handed Barry a few typed pages folded length-wise. He slipped them into his inner blazer pocket without looking at them.

Cookie Crumbles

"Mother, if you continue this asinine assault it will be you who exposes our family to ridicule. Were you planning on bribing Samantha here to disappear in a puff of stage fog to complete your little drama?"

"I thought she'd have the decency to do the right thing."

"I'll tell you what the right thing is. I want you to turn around and return to your table. Then I will make every effort to pretend the last few minutes never happened."

Mrs. Burke stood frozen for a long second. I swear I could feel the sweep hand of the grandfather clock opposite the rest room doors vibrate as it wrested itself from inertia to continue it's rounds. Her lips twitched, a very nearly visible stream of air jetted and she spun away from Barry, on the ball of her foot by the way, not the heel. I began to breathe again.

"Samantha, I want you to know that she isn't quite the harridan she appears to be. I would be forever grateful if you kept this little horror show between us. I plan on being Betsy's husband for a long time and her having a poisoned relationship with my mother from the very start would make our lives more complicated than need be."

"Hurting Betsy is the last thing I would want, consider it forgotten."

"I do have to tell you that I was not thrilled when Betsy told me you were going to be her Maid of Honor, but I understand the bond you two have…Thank you for your kindness." Barry said before he turned to walk away.

I blurted out. "One second! The blond usher…"

"Mike?"

"I guess so, is he family?"

"My mother's nephew, why?"

"Oh, no reason…"

Barry arched an eyebrow and left me to my impure thoughts.

The next day the wedding went off perfectly. There were no glitches, hiccups, or missed cues. Betsy was radiant and Barry looked every bit the perfect groom that Betsy deserved. I was on my best behavior and while I

Cookie Crumbles

did dance with Mike--I couldn't very well turn him down, could I?--I made my way to my room alone as soon as the bride and groom left for their honeymoon. Betsy never found out about my confrontation with her mother-in-law.

The years we spent apart after the wedding attenuated our connections and there were times that we wouldn't speak for months. Careers, family concerns and the computer revolution somehow facilitated seemingly random movements across the country like the little silver ball in Tommy's pinball wizard opera.

Eventually the three of us found ourselves in the same tony suburb of Chicagoland. A few months after reconnecting, Betsy excitedly called to tell me that the townhouse next door was going on the market. Turned out the price was right.

Betsy was infectious, like a virus that bored into your heart and started reproducing her enthusiasms, letting you see things in a way you never would have considered prior to her sharing her vision. The years that had passed since we were at college together dried like thin translucent slices of amber and faded away.

We picked up right where we left off in Madison. We got on our bicycles and learned all the paths and back roads until we could get almost anywhere in town without risking our lives on high traffic thoroughfares. She got me back in tiptop physical shape in less than a year. She discovered that a few homeowners who feared two wheeled thieves would burgle their homes were blocking completion of a north/south trail that would connect the whole city. One by one she talked them into dropping their opposition and the path was finally finished. She was unstoppable.

Betsy never worried about herself. She was always much more concerned about her friends, specifically me. She really thought I needed a man in my life, to settle down, and live happily ever after. There were numerous boyfriends. More than a few were setups that she engineered. Some of them lasted, but when they left, there was always Betsy to hold

Cookie Crumbles

me while I cried. She was my best friend, my sister, and sometimes my mother. And then she was gone.

❖❖❖

Picking up my newspaper and an apple fritter at the Seven/Eleven one morning I heard that Barry and Linda--an involuntary shudder rippled my shoulder blades just to hear the woman's name--had left the previous day on a six week Mediterranean cruise. Linda had been Barry's office manager and was a source of great comfort to him in the eight months that it took a virulent brain tumor to suck the life out of Betsy. That was two years ago and in the interim Linda had managed to fill Barry's entire field of vision until he was blind to everything else including his now sixteen-year-old son, Frankie.

As those months passed and I had become used to riding alone, the ache in my heart faded. I never stopped missing her, but at least I stopped expecting to see her wave to me when I left my house, that was a balm of sorts.

Whenever I peddled home from the Korean nail shop located in one of the strip malls that appear like mushrooms on dead logs in the dim light of morning, I had to traverse a short distance on the state highway itself as it bore through an unincorporated section of McMansions that had fought off annexation--presumably to avoid the heavy expense of those darn sidewalks, among other things.

One day I felt, and then heard the roar of Barry and Betsy's little red Corvette behind me. It was a beautiful machine, as pristine as the day it rolled off the assembly line at GM in 1968. I had walked past the garage dozens of times as Barry worked at restoring the badly decomposed car that he and Betsy had found in a barn in Missouri; tracking down it's rumored existence from a swap meet they'd attended in St. Louis. It was

Cookie Crumbles

his dream car, the one that got away, he'd owned one briefly, but sold it for grad school expenses and in the press of career and family he'd never gotten back to his passion for 'Vettes. That is until Betsy had diagnosed the ennui that had dragged her wonderful man into a morose place that never found any wholesome distraction anymore and set him the task, the quest really, of recreating his little red Corvette. She was such an angel.

The street leading into our cul de sac [Cul de sac, French no? It sounds so much more charming than circular dead end] was fast approaching. I assumed the 'Vette was being piloted by Frankie since by now Barry was somewhere in the Med on a Greek cruise ship. He swung out into the oncoming traffic lane to give me a wide berth, and then punched the accelerator while cocking the little steering wheel too far to the right. The Corvette has an incredibly tight steering ratio, all movements are magnified, the combination of oversteering and acceleration sent the car into a violent fishtail, followed by a horrendous nosedive that scraped the paint off the bottom of the front end to the tune of about 2000 bucks as Frankie stood on the brakes. When he released them the car proceeded to slam into the curb on the far side of the street.

I threw the bike down and sprinted over to the car, of course he hadn't been wearing a seat belt and had bounced around the cockpit a bit, but seemed coherent.

"You OK," I asked?

"Yeah."

"Keep this up and you're gonna kill yourself."

"My old man will take care of that." He answered.

"I take it your Dad said to leave the car in the garage?"

"Whatever…"

"You should have done that! Listen…there are a lot of kids in this neighborhood. And you obviously can't handle this car."

In response he glared at me and restarted the engine that had choked out when he impacted the curb. He crammed it into reverse and floored

Cookie Crumbles

the gas pedal, the car leaped backwards and I jumped a little, I'll admit being frightened. He had to brake really hard before he could put it in first and head toward the opening garage at his house.

"Slow down!" I screeched at him as he rolled away flipping me off.

Frankie made himself scarce after the curb incident, I didn't hear the coming or going of the 'Vette either. I wondered if Frankie would attempt to get the damage to the car fixed before Barry came home. Even though it was extremely minor as car accidents go I knew it would still cost way more to fix it than a sixteen year old could muster. As I opened the overhead garage door, ready to roll my bicycle down to the street I thought of the very first vehicle accident Frankie had been involved in and how I'd always felt guilty about it.

It was a long time ago, Betsy had wanted to restart her journalism career after having given birth and devoting herself to her baby. A local daily had called her in for an interview. She asked me if I could watch Frankie for a couple of hours. What trouble could I have with a five year old I thought? The kid and I had a good relationship, at least as far as ice cream cones and McDonalds french fries.

Moonshine runners have a getaway technique called a bootleg turn where you can do a 180 and head back the way your pursuer came from, the idea being that by the time the Revenue agent gets turned around you are long gone, just like the Duke boys in the General Lee. Ever since the invention of the all-plastic Big Wheel big kids have taught little kids how to do a bootleg. Peddle that front wheel for all your worth until you suddenly freeze the pedals and throw your weight as hard as you can to the right, the rear end rises up slightly and the front wheel acts as a pivot, you fly around and land in a hard, but controlled skid and you take off in the opposite direction. At day care Frankie had been watching an older boy execute the maneuver over and over and now it was his time. He told me he was going to ride his Big Wheel in my driveway, so I kicked off my rope heeled wedgie sandals, curled up with a copy of Vanity Fair and

Cookie Crumbles

settled in to watch.

Frankie rolled in a big lazy figure eight as he warmed up. After a few dozen circuits, OK--only three, he decided to demonstrate the bootleg. I could tell because he shouted, "Watch me, watch me!" He was smart enough to add gravity to his speed, tearing down the driveway's slight incline to the street he executed the bootleg to perfection, magazine forgotten I leaped up and clapped as if I was at a Bruce Springsteen concert. If he had stopped with just the one it would have been a lovely memory but like all of us he thought more is better. Frankie pedaled up to the garage and tore back down toward the street.

A very unfortunate aspect of the construction crew that paved our street was their lack of attention to detail, my understanding was that they were supposed to put curb cuts in at the driveways but it just never happened. On Frankie's second bootleg demo he did not complete his controlled skid before the Big Wheel, still rolling backwards, went over the high curb at an awkward angle and dumped him, head first into the street. As I started running to him, he picked himself off the pavement in what appeared to be a full-throated scream, but could not catch his breath so no sound came out. There was a gash that traversed his hairline at an angle and the blood was pouring down. It would take seven stitches at the ER to close it.

❖❖❖

At the end of another day's errands, I made my way home on my least favorite segment of the trip, that highway, with no real shoulder to speak of, merely a white stripe on my left and a bit of asphalt, solid at first but then rapidly crumbling at the right edge as the surface turns completely to sharp-edged gravel. I was careful to keep up my speed and still avoid getting caught in the dangerous ruts. Finally nearing my turn-off, I saw in the middle distance, a goose standing alone just inside the traffic lane. The buzz of cars and trucks was beginning to thicken for the rush hour and I

Cookie Crumbles

was concerned that she was going to get hurt if she stood there much longer.

As I approached her I saw that there was a large sack beside her. My heart rose to my throat as I considered what it might be, what it must be and I felt my eyes water uncontrollably when I was faced with the confirmation of my worst fear. The sack was indeed the lifeless form of her mate. I jumped off my bicycle and knelt down, talking soothingly to her. I reached out to touch him--she made no move or sound to stop me. He was already turning cold, his neck was broken, his head crushed and bloody, but not all the red was blood, there were flakes of candy apple red paint as well. That discovery made my blood run cold.

I knew that she would not leave his side and so I was faced with the unpleasant duty of moving his body out of the traffic lane so she would not be run over as well. Disregarding my immaculate Korean manicure, I slipped my hands under him and carefully lifted him up as I regained my feet. I moved him fully into the grass at the side of the highway. She followed me closely; still she had not made a sound. I did not know what else to do.

✧✧✧

I pedaled like a woman possessed. I knew with cold certainty exactly what I would find. The Corvette sat cock-eyed on the circle in front of Betsy's house. I squeezed the caliper brakes as though I was angry with them and the bike went into a skid that only ended as I bounced off the driver side door. I went to my knees and examined the right end of the front bumper. It was sticky with blood and a few remnants of black feathers. Frankie had killed the goose in his utter contempt for those people around him; these last two years had changed a sweet lovable boy into, what? I didn't have words for it; in my mind he could have just as easily killed an errant child.

Cookie Crumbles

I was enraged. I ran to the kitchen door. It was locked. I pounded on it so hard my right hand stung and was already turning bright red.

"Frankie, open this door! Right now!"

There was no answer. The upper half of the door was actually four triangular pieces of glass set in a wooden X frame. I went to the flower garden and pulled a decorative brick out of the ground with the intention of smashing the right side glass insert and flipping the lock to open. I took the time to brush the dirt off it. Didn't want to make a mess. The mental image of the set of keys that Betsy had given to me eons ago finally floated up from long-term storage and penetrated the red fog that had enveloped my mind. I dropped the brick and crossed the lawn to my kitchen and retrieved the keys from the junk drawer.

The house was silent, as was I, since I was wearing what my mother always called tennies even though I never held a racket in my life. I figured I'd head for the basement since the neighborhood gossip was that Frankie rarely came upstairs since Linda had moved in. There was a laundry room right off the bottom of the stairs, an exercise room beyond that and Barry's computer lab as well.

At the farthest corner I found Frankie wearing a headset, staring at a giant flat screen firing a laser weapon at some drooling, hulking Bug Eyed Monsters, BEMs they were called when I was his age devouring science fiction books. As the laser burned a hole in the creature it would howl in pain, grimace horrifically and swear revenge against all humans. Gallons of pus and offal would pour out onto the ground and the BEM, like a Macy's Thanksgiving parade balloon, would collapse into a little pile of mottled green and black scaly skin. He was mowing them down.

"Frankie! Turn around!"

When the sound of my strangled voice penetrated his consciousness he stood to his full height and slowly turned to face me.

"What do you want?" He asked flatly without affect.

"I want you to face your responsibility! You killed a living, breathing

Cookie Crumbles

creature.   For no reason other than sheer negligence. Don't you have any remorse? You obviously weren't being careful. How fast were you going? I told you this could happen, it could have been a child that you killed. Do you even care?"

"It was just a damn goose."

My chest was heaving and my eyes were filling with tears. I could not believe this thoughtless, uncaring young man was birthed from Betsy's body.

"Do you think your mother would be proud of you right now? And I'm not just talking about the poor dead goose. I know losing your mom was the worst thing that ever happened to you, but you can't let it ruin the rest of your life. There is a gaping hole in your heart and it feels like it will never heal, believe me I know how you feel, but you have to stop indulging this poisonous attitude you've been wallowing in. You still have your father, he'll always be there for you!"

"Really? My father abandoned me before I was born!"

"What the hell are you talking about?" I asked, genuinely mystified.

"My mother was dying and my father was fucking Linda, that slut! I was so pissed off that I wanted to kill him, but Mom told me I had to forgive him, that he was just a man. He couldn't deal with losing her, watching her die by inches so he was moving on, walling her off by hiding behind Linda. But when he moved her into my mother's house I lost it! I went ballistic on him. We were screaming at each other, I hit him!"

"You what?" I was stunned at this admission.

"I HIT him. And it felt good. I said that I didn't want him as my father anymore."

Frankie was shaking, his face was flushed scarlet and tears were coursing down his cheeks now. I took a step closer toward him.

Frankie continued "He looked at me, he said 'Works for me you little piece of shit, you've never--ever--been my son! Do you know why? Your biological father is your mother's gal pal Samantha, only back in college

Cookie Crumbles

she was Sam her gay best friend. Go on, ask HER about it!'"

I reached out to Frankie and placed my hands on his shoulders.

"It's true, I provided the sperm that…"

He twisted out of my grasp, "Take your hands off me you goddamn faggot, I hate you too. FUCK YOU! FUCK ALL OF YOU!"

I will regret the next second for as long as I draw breath. Without any volition my right hand drew back and slashed the air leaving a red print on Frankie's face. We were both already crying, I begged his forgiveness, but I was talking to empty air. He was gone from the rec room and a second later I heard the roar of the 'Vette as it drove away.

I went back to my kitchen. I felt like my hair was on fire. I was beyond angry and I had too many targets--Frankie, Barry, God, even Betsy but most of all, myself. I couldn't believe I'd hit him; I'm just not the violent type. But he'd driven me past my limits.

I cursed my decision to allow Betsy to use the sperm I'd frozen before I had my gender reassignment surgery in Colorado. Betsy had come to me, she was desperate to have a child but all the tests showed that Barry was sterile; the results were incontrovertible. She said she didn't want some stranger's sperm; she didn't want to play craps with her child's future. If only I had said no, I wouldn't have had this terrible secret knowledge and worse, this terrible moral responsibility with no legal standing to take control.

I walked to the freezer and put a few ice cubes in my empty cocktail glass, pulled out a frosty bottle of tequila and poured three fingers onto the ice. I sat down at the dinette and considered my options, which were, as the movie cowboys used to say, slim and none; and slim just rode out of town.

I needed my lawyer. He was the kind of shark you called when the cops caught you standing over a corpse with the blood-dripping knife still in your hand.

This situation was deadly serious, a boy's life hung in the balance,

Cookie Crumbles

Frankie was my flesh and blood and my pledge of omerta to Betsy was now null and void. He was being emotionally hollowed out by Barry's indifference. I wasn't going to abandon this child who I had remotely fathered.

Up to now I could hide behind the idea that Barry had promised Betsy he would raise him and love him as his own, but the truth had shredded that little conceit. Frankie was my son and I had to rescue him. I picked up my cell phone; punched in my lawyer's number and listened to the ringing.

Cookie Crumbles

Miss Cookie Crumbles is a drag performer, writer, performance artist and a damn fine cook. She was born beyond the Cheddar Curtain but moved south during the Cretaceous Period. She sleeps in Naperville, IL and lives in Chicago and Oak Park. She also enjoys spending her holidays in New Orleans collecting beads, doubloons, recipes, viruses and story ideas. Thanks to her association with Chicago's NewTown Writers she has had the opportunity to perform in many stage shows over the past seven years. The picture displayed on the rear cover is from her role as "Coral Reef" in the production of James Wilke's hilarious one act play titled "Undercover Queens." She hopes if you enjoy this book you'll tell all your friends and if you don't she hopes you'll lie to them.

Cookie Crumbles

Cookie Crumbles